Stephanie Smith (formerly Lovegrove) is a barrister at 4-5 Gray's Inn Square specialising in Housing, Landlord and Tenant and related Local Government and Property law. She has over 20 years of experience acting for and advising both landlords and tenants in residential and commercial property related matters, including service charge disputes, enfranchisement, the right to manage and the appointment of managers.

Stephanie is ranked in both Chambers and Partners and the Legal 500 where she has been described as "demonstrating prowess across all areas of Landlord and Tenant law", "absolutely excellent: clients and solicitors love her alike", and it is said that her "meticulous attention to detail, combined with her deep understanding of housing law, ensures that every aspect of a case is thoroughly examined and expertly argued".

A Practical Guide to the Appointment of Managers for Leasehold Flats

A Practical Guide to the Appointment of Managers for Leasehold Flats

Stephanie Smith
Barrister, Lincoln's Inn
BA (Hons) (Oxon)

Law Brief Publishing

Published 2025 by Law Brief Publishing, an imprint of Law Brief Publishing Ltd
30 The Parks
Minehead
Somerset
TA24 8BT

www.lawbriefpublishing.com

Paperback: 978-1-916698-86-4

For Alexandra

PREFACE

Some have accused me of writing Practical Guides on the "drier" areas of law: Succession to Social Housing Tenancies... Unlawful Eviction and Harassment... twice.

My response is uniform. The law I'm interested in (Housing) is probably a fair bit less exciting than white collar fraud, corporate takeovers or murder, but its day-to-day impact on someone's ability to enjoy their home and everything that comes with that is felt across the years. Across generations. These issues affect our families, our finances, our mental health, our own internal sense of comfort and respect. The areas of law may be dry, but their effect is potentially life-altering.

The law of appointment of a manager is no different. Living in a block of flats with warring landlords, tenants and managing agents may not invoke the guerrilla images of conflict we see on the news (one hopes!), but these conflicts can have a massive impact on people's lives. Anything that can be done to ensure the homes, investments and inheritances of ordinary people are well-maintained at a fair cost and managed in a way to build communities rather than create discord is to be welcomed and used.

I hope this book, if not enjoyable, is at least helpful at walking you through this complex subject.

The law stated in this book is believed to be correct based on information available to me as at 7th April 2025.

Stephanie Smith
April 2025

CONTENTS

CHAPTER ONE

INTRODUCTION

In *Cawsand Fort Management Co Limited v Stafford* [2007] 1 E.G.L.R. 85 Mummery LJ stated (at [31]) that the practical purpose of the appointment of a manager is:

> "to protect the interests of the lessees of premises which form part of the building, by enabling them to secure, through the flexible discretionary machinery of the appointment of a manager, the carrying out of the management functions which they are entitled to enjoy 'in relation to' the premises of which their flats are part".

This book seeks to give potential applicant leaseholders in England and Wales a practical guide to applying for an order from the First-Tier Tribunal (in England) or Leasehold Valuation Tribunal (in Wales) for the appointment of a manager to manage the property and surrounding areas of which their flat forms part.

The law about this area is primarily governed by Part II, Landlord and Tenant Act 1987.

The right to apply for the appointment of a manager has existed since 1988 but it remains a less well-known and under-utilised way of addressing concerns about the management of properties comprising leasehold flats. The more familiar "right to manage" tends to be the first port of call for leaseholders and this book will explore what advantages there may be to having a manager appointed rather than having leaseholders directly take on obligations under the lease via a right to manage company in Chapter 7.

The right to apply for the appointment of a manager is a fault-based right designed to replace the persons managing the property under the terms of the lease (whether a landlord, a right to manage company, a management company under the terms of the relevant lease or a receiver) with an alternative manager. The hope underpinning the right is that whoever replaces the incumbent management does a better job at performing those obligations and for better value for money.

It is important to recognise at this early stage that whilst there is a right for leaseholders to apply for the appointment of a manager, it is the appropriate tribunal (whether the FTT, LVT or Upper Tribunal) that decides whether the fault-based grounds for making such an appointment are satisfied and, even if they are so satisfied, has a discretion whether to make the appointment or not.

This book comprises seven chapters including an introduction and conclusion: chapters two and three look at what a manager is in context and when the right applies; the fourth considers the grounds for appointment and the exercise of the Tribunal's discretion including what evidence is needed to support an application; the fifth chapter considers the procedure for applying, and hearings and decision-making in the tribunal, and the penultimate chapter looks at what happens if management does not improve or gets worse under the appointment.

It is hoped that you will feel confident deciding whether the appointment of a manager is appropriate in the circumstances of your case and if necessary embarking on and navigating the process of applying for that appointment.

CHAPTER TWO

WHAT IS A MANAGER?

I think it is fair to say that most people, when asked what a manager of a block of flats was, would come up with something along the lines of a managing agent: a person who takes on the responsibility of managing the repairs, complaints and other day-to-day responsibilities of the landlord under the terms of the leases of those flats. Such a managing agent is, as the name implies, the agent of the landlord and ultimate responsibility for the discharge of the obligations remains with the landlord.

Many people may not appreciate that their leases may separate the obligations of the landlord as the freehold owner of the block from the responsibilities for repair of the block, maintenance of any estate, collection of rents and service charges and general management which are carried out by a management company as a third party to the lease. This occurs in what are known as "tripartite" leases involving (1) a lessor or landlord, (2) a leaseholder or lessee and (3) a management company. This arrangement is not quite the same as that involving a managing agent because the management company has its own specific obligations under the lease and can be sued directly by the other parties to the lease for any failure to comply.

A manager appointed by a Tribunal is more than either of these things.

The leading case on this area is that of *Maunder Taylor v Blaquiere* [2002] EWCA Civ 1633; [2003] 1 W.L.R. 379. In this case the lessee occupied a flat under a lease containing repair and redecoration covenants which the landlords breached. The landlords did not remedy the defects and did not appear to intend to do so; as a result, the tenant applied for the appointment of a manager. The LVT (as it then was called in England) granted the application and Mr Maunder Taylor was appointed the manager. He claimed service charges from the tenants in order to do the repair and redecoration work. The tenant counterclaimed damages to be set off against the service charges on the basis that the manager owed the tenant the same duties of repair as the landlords under the underlease. The judge at first instance held that there was no ability to set off damages for disrepair against a tribunal appointed manager because (1) the effect of appointing a manager was not that the manager stepped into the landlord's shoes such that he assumed contractual responsibility for the performance of the landlord's covenants under the lease; and (2) whilst the claims were sufficiently directly connected to give rise to a right of set-off in equity, it was not just and equitable to allow it in the circumstances (i.e., where a manager was appointed at tenants' behest, to carry out the obligations of a landlord who had neglected the same, and the manager needed to call in service charges to get those obligations performed).

The Court of Appeal upheld the decision of the judge below albeit the reasons given were different. Giving the unanimous decision of the Court, Aldous LJ held the following from p.392:

> "38 […] the purpose of Part II of the Act is to enable the tribunal to appoint a manager, who may not be confined to carrying out the duties of a landlord under a lease. The tribunal is enabled under subsection (1) to appoint a manager to carry out in relation to any premises to which Part II applies "such functions in connection with management" of the premises as the tribunal thinks fit. It is to be noted that the premises may be two or more (see section 21(4)) and that the manager will carry out functions of management. As subsection (11) makes clear, that includes repair, maintenance or

insurance. There is no limitation as to the management functions of the manager; in particular the functions are not limited to carrying out the terms of the leases. That is not surprising as the manager will need to obtain estimates and do repairs. He need not use the landlord's surveyor as required by the lease in this case.

39 [...] [T]he tribunal is concerned to provide a scheme of management not just a manager of the landlord's obligations [...].

41 In my view the purpose of Part II of the 1987 Act is to provide a scheme for the appointment of a manager who will carry out the functions required by the court. That manager carries out those functions in his own right as a court-appointed official. He is not appointed as the manager of the landlord or even of the landlord's obligations under the lease. That being so, Mr Maunder Taylor was a court-appointed manager appointed to carry out those duties required by the order appointing him. He did not carry on the business of [the landlord]. His claims were made in his capacity as manager.

42 [...] The manager acts in a capacity independent of the landlord. In this case the duties and liabilities laid down in the order are defined by reference to the lease, but do not alter his capacity. In my view Mr Maunder Taylor's right to the money claimed arose from his appointment not from the lease. It follows that there was no mutuality between his claim and that of [the tenant]. That being so, set-off is not possible.

> 43 […] Further, it must be possible for the manager to obtain funds necessary to manage the property even though the tenants, or some of them, had a right to refuse further payment, e g where they have paid and the landlord has absconded with the money. In such a case the tribunal decides the rights. Their jurisdiction is not confined to the terms of the lease. Part II envisages interim appointments, when action needs to be taken urgently. If so, the possibility of a set-off could obstruct that which Parliament intended Part II of the Act to achieve. Section 24 provides a mechanism for appointing a suitable person to manage the functions of flats when needed with the rights as needed."

Longmore LJ added at p.393:

> "50 It is clear to my mind that Parliament intended that a manager should, when appointed pursuant to section 24(1) of the Act, come in with a clean sheet and be able to collect service charges due from the tenants and use the money so obtained for repair of the premises. It would make a nonsense of the legislation if any or all of the tenants could set off, against that claim for service charges, claims that they might have against the landlord. Most tenants would have such claims. Some of those claims will have accrued before the appointment of their manager; other claims may be for continuing breaches and thus continue to accrue after the manager's appointment. Mr Blaquiere elected to confine his claims in the present litigation to claims in the latter category. But the logic of his argument

> applies to claims in both categories. In my judgment, the use of such claims to prevent service charges being paid to the manager would be an attempt to thwart the plain legislative intent displayed in the relevant sections of Part II of the 1987 Act."

So, the duties of a tribunal appointed manager are not confined to those of the landlord under the terms of the lease or statute. The tribunal's order decides the nature and extent of the manager's duties and powers albeit they can be defined by reference to the terms of the lease. The appointment of a manager does not have the effect of "suspending" or "disapplying" the obligations of the landlord which remain. A failure to carry out repairs would not prevent a leaseholder from suing the landlord for breach of the landlord's covenant for repair under the terms of the lease for example.

It has been acknowledged in subsequent cases that the jurisdiction under Part II of the 1987 Act is a problem-solving jurisdiction: *Chuan-Hui v. K Group Holdings Inc.* [2021] EWCA Civ 403 at [29]. The aim is to put in place a properly functioning system of management and not merely to replace the landlord with someone more capable for the purpose of discharging only the landlord's or management company's lease obligations: see e.g., *Kol v Bowring* [2015] UKUT 530 (LC).

The effect of this is that the appointment of a manager can cure defects in the lease such as an inability to collect service charges for want of adequate provision in the lease, to ensure proper apportionment of service charges where the percentages do not add up or to include properties which are not demised in the contribution.

It is apparent from the above that a tribunal appointed manager is more than a managing agent or even a "substitute" landlord or management company. The manager can be monitored by the tribunal, directed to do things like repairs as specified in the tribunal's order or – on subsequent direction from the tribunal, and expected to follow all proper professional codes of practice and use all income derived from the service charge for the management of the property.

Leaseholder nomination

When making the application for the appointment of a manager, leaseholders must complete a section of the form (detailed later) which nominates a manager for appointment. This is likely to be a professional managing agent and that agent is more likely to be appointed if they have some experience of tribunal appointment already. That said, there may be circumstances where a tribunal will appoint a manager without professional qualifications: e.g., *Howard v Midrome Ltd* [1991] 1 EGLR 58. That is not to say that the leaseholders themselves cannot ask to be appointed as a manager, and some do, facilitated by setting up a limited company for that purpose. That company if approved can then appoint a professional managing agent.

The manager will be expected to evidence their suitability for appointment and so leaseholders should begin an exercise of assessment of who will be nominated early on in the process. The nominated manager will need to show their credentials, understanding of the role especially as an officer of the tribunal and knowledge of all relevant codes of management practice. They will need to confirm their willingness to act in accordance with the tribunal's direction and the codes. If they are a professional managing agent, they will also need to possess adequate indemnity insurance.

POINTS TO NOTE:

- A tribunal appointed manager does not step into the shoes of the landlord. They are a court appointed manager and their powers are freestanding and not derived from the terms of the lease. Accordingly, for example, they can make charges for services separately from the service charge mechanism in the lease.

- A manager cannot be sued in their personal capacity for the landlord's failures under the lease whether historic or post appointment.

- The applicants for an order must be able to identify a manager they wish to nominate for appointment at an early stage (i.e., when the application is made).

- The characteristics and experience of a manager is set out in the tribunal's helpful Practice Direction annexed to this book.

CHAPTER THREE

WHEN DOES THE RIGHT TO APPLY TO APPOINT A MANAGER ARISE?

There are various criteria that must be met in order for the right to apply to appoint a manager to arise. Absent satisfying all of the statutory criteria, the tribunal simply does not have the jurisdiction to make the order sought.

The criteria can be broken down into the following:

(1) The tenant criteria,

(2) The premises criteria,

(3) The landlord exemptions, and

(4) The preliminary notice requirement.

The tenant criteria

In order to qualify for the right to apply for the appointment of a manager, the tenant must satisfy the requirements of s.21 of the 1987 Act. Section 21(1) provides:

> "(1) The tenant of a flat contained in any premises to which this Part applies may, subject to the following provisions of this Part, apply to the appropriate tribunal for an order under section 24

> appointing a manager to act in relation to those premises."

"Tenancy" is defined in s.60(1) of the 1987 Act as *including* a statutory tenancy – itself defined as a tenancy under the Rent Act 1977 or the Rent (Agriculture) Act 1976. This does not preclude long-leaseholders or other forms of tenancy, which is reinforced by the fact that tenants under business tenancies under Part II, Landlord and Tenant Act 1954 are specifically excluded by s.21(7) which provides:

> "(7) References in this Part to a tenant do not include references to a tenant under a tenancy to which Part II of the Landlord and Tenant Act 1954 applies."

Whilst this excludes tenancies of flats used for business purposes or mixed-use flats (where premises are occupied for mixed business and residential purposes, the tenancy is likely to be one to which the Landlord and Tenant Act 1954, Pt II applies: see *Cheryl Investments v Saldanha* [1978] 1 WLR 1329), it is relatively straightforward to cease use as business premises and therefore fall within the qualification criteria to exercise the right under s.24.

The tenant must be a tenant of a "flat". "Flat" is defined in s.60(1) of the 1987 Act as:

> "a separate set of premises whether or not on the same floor:
>
> (a) which forms part of a building;
>
> (b) which is divided horizontally from some other part of that building; and

(c) which is constructed or adapted for use for the purposes of a dwelling.

"Dwelling" means a building or part of a building occupied or intended to be occupied as a separate dwelling (with or without appurtenances – meaning rights or privileges linked to the use of the flat such as a garage, storage space or parking rights): s.60(1) of the 1987 Act.

There are several cases which look at what counts as a flat under other related legislation which contain almost the same definition of a flat, namely the 2002 Act and the Leasehold Reform, Housing and Urban Development Act 1993. In *Aldford House Freehold Ltd v Grosvenor (Mayfair) Estate* [2019] EWCA Civ 1848; [2020] Ch. 270, Lewison LJ held the following regarding the definition in the context of a claim for enfranchisement of the freehold under the 1993 Act. On the issue of "separate premises" he held (at [17] and [19]):

> "the relevant question is whether there was or was not physical separation between the various spaces [...] the physical separation between the areas was enough for each area to amount to a "separate" set of premises. The fact that the separation was potentially reversible with little effort does not, in my judgment, mean that the two areas were not in fact separate on the relevant date."

On the issue of construction or adaptation for the purposes of a dwelling, his Lordship considered definitions in other statutory contexts and cases about what types of buildings fell within them and concluded as follows in the context of words identical to that in the 1987 Act:

> "If a putative flat is in the course of construction, it has not yet been 'constructed' for any purpose. Second, whereas a house must be designed 'for living in', a flat must be constructed "for use for the purposes of a dwelling". This is more than simply requiring that a flat must be constructed for the purposes of a dwelling. It must be constructed for use for that purpose. A purpose may be a future purpose. But if a separate set of premises is to be constructed 'for use' as a dwelling, it must, in my judgment, be in a state in which it is suitable for use as a dwelling. [...] Mr Jourdan accepted that in a case of adaptation rather than construction, there had to be some physical work which changed the previous identity of the premises from something that was not suitable for use as a dwelling to something that was. I cannot see any warrant for different tests being applied to the constituent parts of the definition. Accordingly, in my judgment the same meaning should be ascribed to that word in that part of the definition of 'flat' which refers to 'construction ... for use for the purposes of a dwelling'".

On the issue of what is meant by "dwelling", Lewison LJ drew upon the decision in *Uratemp Ventures Ltd v Colliers* [2001] UKHL 43; [2002] 1 A.C. 301 in which the then House of Lords held (per Lord Irvine at [3]) that the word "dwelling" for the purposes of the Housing Act 1988 was:

> "[...] not a term of art, but a familiar word in the English language, which, in my judgment, in this context, connotes a place where one lives, regarding and treating it as home. Such a place does not cease

> to be a "dwelling" merely because one takes all or some of one's meals out, or brings in takeaway food to the exclusion of home cooking, or, at times, prepares some food for consumption on heating devices falling short of a full cooking facility.
>
> Decisions on the infinite factual variety of cases are for judges of trial, and their decisions on the facts of individual cases should neither be treated, nor cited, as propositions of law. I would not myself, for example, regard a bed, any more than cooking facilities, as an essential prerequisite of a "dwelling": every case is for the judge of trial, but I would have no difficulty with a conclusion that one could live in a room that is regarded and treated as home, although taking one's sleep, without the luxury of a bed, in an armchair or in blankets on the floor."

Furthermore, in *JLK Ltd and others v Ezekwe* [2017] UKUT 277 (LC), Martin Roger QC, having considered the meaning of "separate dwelling" for the purposes of the jurisdiction to determine service charge payments under the Landlord and Tenant Act 1985 held the following:

> "51. [...] The requirement of section 38 that, to be a 'dwelling' to which sections 18 to 30 of the 1985 Act apply, the house or part of a house must be intended to be occupied as a 'separate' dwelling, is not modified in the 1985 Act so as to enable the sharing of living accommodation with another person to be disregarded.
>
> 52. I do not consider that it is possible to interpret section 38 of the 1985 Act without regard to

> meaning which has been given to the expression "as a separate dwelling" for the purpose of the Rent Acts and the Housing Act 1988.
>
> 53. It is therefore necessary to consider the effect of the shared living accommodation at Alexander Terrace. The tenant of each of the units has the right to share a kitchen, lounge, shower and w.c. with every other tenant on the same floor. Can it then be said that the tenant is the tenant of a part of the building which is occupied or intended to be occupied as a separate dwelling? I do not think it can, for the reasons given by Lord Reid in *Baker v Turner*. The bed-sitting room plus the right to use the communal space will not satisfy the requirement because the tenant is not tenant of the whole of that accommodation, but only of part of it; the bed-sitting room itself will not do, because that is not occupied as the tenant's dwelling, but only as part of it. That was the conclusion reached by the FTT in the *St Andrews Place* case, and in my judgment it was correct."

Accordingly, in order to be a "flat" as defined, it is necessary that the "dwelling" be separate and therefore the sharing of a kitchen, lounge, bathroom and/or toilet will prevent the premises occupied from being "flats" for the purposes of s.60(1) of the 1987 Act. There are some authorities which appear to go the other way, but the approach in *Ezekwe* was followed in *Q Studios (Stoke) RTM Co Ltd v Premier Grounds Rents No.6 Ltd and another* [2020] UKUT 197 (LC) where permission to appeal the decision was refused by the Court of Appeal.

Importantly, "tenant" is capable of including a landlord where the application is made against a right to manage company. The

Commonhold and Leasehold Reform Act 2002 introduced the concept of a "right to manage" which, broadly, enables tenants of flats to band together as a company to take over many of the landlord's rights and obligations under the terms of the lease. Where an RTM Co. has taken over those rights and obligations, Part II of the 1987 Act is modified by Schedule 7, paragraph 8 of the 2002 Act as follows so far as material:

> "(1) Part 2 of the 1987 Act (appointment of manager by . . . tribunal) has effect with the modifications provided by this paragraph.
>
> (2) References to the landlord are to the RTM company.
>
> (3) References to a tenant of a flat contained in the premises include a person who is landlord under a lease of the whole or any part of the premises.
>
> (4)-(8) [...]"

So, the script is semantically flipped when an RTM Co. is involved in order to ensure the right to appoint a manager is made available to those who are not managing the premises concerned.

Section 21(4) states:

> "(4) An application for an order under section 24 may be made—
>
> (a) jointly by tenants of two or more flats if they are each entitled to make such an application by virtue of this section, and

> (b) in respect of two or more premises to which this Part applies;
>
> and, in relation to any such joint application as is mentioned in paragraph (a), references in this Part to a single tenant shall be construed accordingly."

Section 21(5) states:

> "(5) Where the tenancy of a flat contained in any such premises is held by joint tenants, an application for an order under section 24 in respect of those premises may be made by any one or more of those tenants."

It is apparent from the wording above that joint tenants are specifically treated severally (i.e., as individual separate tenants rather than as one joint tenant). This enables an application to be made by one person out of two or more joint tenants rather than requiring all joint tenants to act "jointly".

It is important to note at this early stage that by s.21(6), where a tenant has the right to apply for the appointment of a manager of premises under s.24 of the 1987 Act, that tenant cannot apply to a court for it to appoint a receiver or manager in relation to those premises.

As discussed in the introduction to this book, by s.21(8), for the purposes of Part II of the 1987 Act, "appropriate tribunal" means, depending on where premises are located, the First-tier Tribunal or, where determined by or under Tribunal Procedure Rules, the Upper Tribunal in England; and the leasehold valuation tribunal in Wales.

The upshot of the above is that, unlike the right to manage under the 2002 Act which requires more than one tenant to apply to exercise the right, the right to apply for the appointment of a manager is exercisable by one tenant (or one of two or more joint tenants) alone. While this is possible, in practical terms, the more tenants making the application and supporting the deficiencies in current management, the stronger and more persuasive the application will be and the more likely it is that it will be successful.

The premises criteria

Section 21(2) provides that

> "(2) Subject to subsection (3) [and section 24ZA], this Part applies to premises consisting of the whole or part of a building if the building or part contains two or more flats."

Subsection (3) states that Part II of the 1987 Act does not apply to any such premises at a time when—

> "(a) the interest of the landlord in the premises is held by—
>
> (i) an exempt landlord or a resident landlord, or
>
> (ii) the Welsh Ministers in their new towns residuary capacity, or
>
> (b) the premises are included within the functional land of any charity."

Subsection (3)(a)(i) is qualified by subsection (3A) as follows:

> "But this Part is not prevented from applying to any premises because the interest of the landlord in the premises is held by a resident landlord if at least one-

> half of the flats contained in the premises are held on long leases which are not tenancies to which Part 2 of the Landlord and Tenant Act 1954 (c 56) applies."

Section 24ZA provides that a special measures manager of a higher-risk building as appointed under paragraph 4 of Schedule 7 of the Building Safety Act 2022 can apply for the appointment of a manager under s.24 and modifies s.24 accordingly.

So, we can glean from the above that the whole of Part II of the 1987 Act (including the scope of a tribunal's orders appointing managers) applies to premises which consist of the whole or part of a building containing two or more flats. Those flats need only be physically there – they need not be demised under a tenancy or occupied.

The right applies as long as:

(1) those premises are not included within the functional land of any charity which s.60(1) of the 1987 Act defines as "land occupied by the charity, or by trustees for it, and wholly or mainly used for charitable purposes";

(2) the interest of the landlord (defined as the immediate landlord or in relation to a statutory tenant the person who apart from the statutory tenancy would be entitled to possession of the premises subject to the tenancy) in the premises is not held by the Welsh Ministers in their new towns residuary capacity;

(3) the interest of the landlord in the premises is not held by an exempt landlord (as for which see below) or a resident landlord. A resident landlord is specified in s.58(2) and (3) as follows:

> "(2) For the purposes of this Act the landlord of any premises consisting of the whole or part of a building is a resident landlord of those premises at any time if—
>
> (a) the premises are not, and do not form part of, a purpose-built block of flats; and
>
> (b) at that time the landlord occupies a flat contained in the premises as his only or principal residence; and
>
> (c) he has so occupied such a flat throughout a period of not less than 12 months ending with that time.
>
> (3) In subsection (2) "purpose-built block of flats" means a building which contained as constructed, and contains, two or more flats."

Subsection (3A) serves to reinclude as qualifying premises those premises where there is a resident landlord but at least one-half of the flats contained in the premises are held on long leases (which are not business tenancies under Part II of the 1954 Act). "Long lease" means a lease for a term in excess of 21 years, a perpetually renewable lease, or a Right to Buy/Right to Acquire lease: s.59(1) of the 1987 Act.

Applications in relation to more than one "premises"

It can be seen from s.21(4)(b) of the 1987 Act, above, that an application to appoint a manager can be made in respect of two or more premises provided they are premises to which the Landlord and Tenant Act 1987, Pt II applies. It must be recalled that premises to which Part II applies are set out in s.21(3), namely those consisting of the whole or part of a building if the building or part contains two or more flats.

So, in order to bring an application in respect of more than one premises, at least one tenant from each building or part thereof containing at least two flats must apply. The purpose behind facilitating applications in relation to more than one set of premises is to ensure management of estates containing separate blocks of flats that all contribute to one service charge fund e.g. can be managed effectively.

The landlord exemptions

As we have seen from s.21(3) of the 1987 Act, Part II does not apply to any qualifying premises at a time when the interest of the landlord in the premises is held by an exempt landlord. The list of exempt landlords is found in s.58(1) of the 1987 Act and includes the following bodies:

(1) a district, county, county borough or London borough council, the Common Council of the City of London, a fire and rescue authority created by an order under section 4A of the Fire and Rescue Services Act 2004, the London Fire Commissioner, the Council of the Isles of Scilly, a police and crime commissioner, the Mayor's Office for Policing and Crime, a joint authority established by Part 4 of the Local Government Act 1985, an economic prosperity board established under section 88 of the Local Democracy, Economic Development and Construction Act 2009, a combined authority established under section 103 of that Act or a combined county authority established under section 9(1) of the Levelling-up and Regeneration Act 2023;

(2) a development corporation established by an order made (or having effect as if made) under the New Towns Act 1981;

(3) a Mayoral development corporation;

(4) an urban development corporation within the meaning of Part XVI of the Local Government, Planning and Land Act 1980;

(5) a housing action trust established under Part III of the Housing Act 1988;

(6) the Broads Authority;

(7) a National Park authority;

(8) the Homes and Communities Agency;

(9) the Greater London Authority so far as exercising its housing or regeneration functions or its new towns and urban development functions;

(10) the Regulator of Social Housing;

(11) a housing trust (as defined in section 6 of the Housing Act 1985) which is a charity;

(12) a non-profit private registered provider of social housing, and, in relation to social housing within the meaning of Part 2 of the Housing and Regeneration Act 2008, a profit-making private registered provider of social housing: see s.58(1ZA).

(13) a registered social landlord (bearing the same meaning as in the Housing Act 1985 (see s.5(4) and (5) of that Act);

(14) a fully mutual housing association (bearing the same meaning as in the Housing Associations Act 1985 (see s.1(1) and (2) of that Act) which is neither a private registered provider of social housing nor a registered social landlord; or

(15) an authority established under section 10 of the Local Government Act 1985 (joint arrangements for waste disposal functions).

The preliminary notice requirement

Section 22 of the 1987 Act imposes a requirement on the tenant who will be applying to the appropriate tribunal to serve a notice containing prescribed content on the landlord (or RTM Co where appropriate) and any other person with management obligations. That notice effectively warns of the impending application and sets out the grounds to be relied on.

Section 22 states:

> "(1) Before an application for an order under section 24 is made in respect of any premises to which this Part applies by a tenant of a flat contained in those premises, a notice under this section must (subject to subsection (3)) be served by the tenant on—
>
> (i) the landlord, and
>
> (ii) any person (other than the landlord) by whom obligations relating to the management of the premises or any part of them are owed to the tenant under his tenancy.

(2) A notice under this section must—

(a) specify the tenant's name, the address of his flat and an address in England and Wales (which may be the address of his flat) at which any person on whom the notice is served may serve notices, including notices in proceedings, on him in connection with this Part;

(b) state that the tenant intends to make an application for an order under section 24 to be made by the appropriate tribunal in respect of such premises to which this Part applies as are specified in the notice, but (if paragraph (d) is applicable) that he will not do so if the requirement specified in pursuance of that paragraph is complied with;

(c) specify the grounds on which the tribunal would be asked to make such an order and the matters that would be relied on by the tenant for the purpose of establishing those grounds;

(d) where those matters are capable of being remedied by any person on whom the notice is served, require him, within such reasonable period as is specified in the notice, to take steps for the purpose of remedying them as are so specified; and

(e) contain such information (if any) as the Secretary of State may by regulations prescribe.

(3) The appropriate tribunal may (whether on the hearing of an application for an order under section 24 or not) by order dispense with the requirement to serve a notice under this section on a person in a

> case where it is satisfied that it would not be reasonably practicable to serve such a notice on the person, but the tribunal may, when doing so, direct that such other notices are served, or such other steps are taken, as it thinks fit.
>
> (4) In a case where—
>
> (a) a notice under this section has been served on the landlord, and
>
> (b) his interest in the premises specified in pursuance of subsection (2)(b) is subject to a mortgage,
>
> the landlord shall, as soon as is reasonably practicable after receiving the notice, serve on the mortgagee a copy of the notice."

The above is broadly pretty self-explanatory.

For the purposes of subsection (2)(d), whether a breach can be remedied depends on whether the harm done by the breach is for practical purposes capable of remedy within a reasonable time: see *Expert Clothing Service and Sales Ltd v Hillgate House Ltd* [1986] Ch 340, [1985] 2 All ER 998, CA.

By s.23 of the 1987 Act,

> "[…] no application for an order under section 24 can be made unless
>
> (a) in a case where a notice has been served under section 22, either—

(i) the period specified in pursuance of paragraph (d) of subsection (2) of that section has expired without the person required to take steps in pursuance of that paragraph having taken them, or

(ii) that paragraph was not applicable in the circumstances of the case; or

(b) in a case where the requirement to serve such a notice has been dispensed with by an order under subsection (3) of that section, either—

(i) any notices required to be served, and any other steps required to be taken, by virtue of the order have been served or (as the case may be) taken, or

(ii) no direction was given by the tribunal when making the order."

It will be seen from the above that there are limited circumstances where the leaseholder can apply to the FTT for an order to dispense with the requirement to serve this preliminary notice on the landlord, for example where the landlord cannot be found.

The notice should ideally be served by hand on the recipient in person or, if this is neither possible nor practicable, by recorded delivery post or with a certificate of posting from the Post Office in order to demonstrate the notice has been served. This should be retained as it may be needed as evidence later in the process. Where the postal service is used, the deemed service provisions in s.7, Interpretation Act 1978 will apply.

There is an example of a preliminary notice on the LEASE website at https://www.lease-advice.org/template-document/preliminary-notice-application-for-the-appointment-of-a-manager-2/ but care should be taken by the tenant to ensure the notice ticks all the statutory requirements in place at the time of service.

The effect of s.23 is that if the landlord etc. complies with the remedial requirements in the notice, the notice has served its purpose and no application under s.24 can be made. It would only be if there were other irremediable bases for bringing the application or the notice requirements were dispensed with and any conditions imposed as part of that dispensation not complied with by the landlord etc. that an application could still be brought.

A "reasonable period for remedy" is similar in meaning to that in relation to forfeiture notices under s.146, Law of Property Act 1925 and depends on the circumstances: a major works project will take longer to undertake than minor repairs to an isolated part of the common areas e.g. Tenants should be careful to factor in any statutory consultation processes that may be required for works in respect of which a service charge is payable under s.20ZA of the Landlord and Tenant Act 1925. Tendering processes and time for specifications to be drawn up must also be factored in.

If there is an error in the preliminary notice, there is no savings provision contained in the 1987 Act and no power to amend or add to the notice. The tribunal can dispense with the notice as mentioned above but only where "it is satisfied that it would not be reasonably practicable to serve such a notice on the landlord". The intended recipient can waive the requirement for notice: see *Riverside CREM 3 Ltd v Unsdorfer* [2022] UKUT 98 (LC) but it is considered unlikely that this would be a regular occurrence.

Accordingly, it is important to ensure that the notice is accurate and clear/unambiguous. There are authorities which are likely to apply in context, the effect of which is to "save" a notice containing an error or omission but only in very limited circumstances. Those circumstances might include applying urgently for an interim order to address a building safety issue, e.g., or where the landlord cannot be found.

In those cases in which the statute confers a property or similar right on a private person and the issue is whether non-compliance with the statutory requirement precludes that person from acquiring the right in question (see *Natt v Osman*), the approach is not one of "substantial compliance" with the statutory requirements but rather (per Etherton C at [31]):

> "[t]he court has interpreted the notice to see whether it actually complies with the strict requirements of the statute; if it does not, then the court has, as a matter of statutory interpretation, held the notice to be wholly valid or wholly invalid."

On the issue of invalidity, Etherton C continued:

> "... the intention of the legislature as to the consequences of non-compliance with the statutory procedures (where not expressly stated in the statute) is to be ascertained in the light of the statutory scheme as a whole."

In *Elim Court RTM Co Ltd v Avon Freeholds Ltd* Lewison LJ held at [52] that:

> "...[w]here the notice or the information which is missing from it is of critical importance in the context of the scheme the non-compliance with the statute will generally result in the invalidity of the notice. Where, on the other hand the information missing from the statutory notice is of secondary importance or merely ancillary, the notice may be held to have been valid ... One useful pointer is

> whether the information required is particularised in the statute as opposed to being required by general provisions of the statute. In the latter case the information is also likely to be viewed as of secondary importance. Another is whether the information is required by the statute itself or by subordinate legislation. In the latter case the information is likely to be viewed as of secondary importance. In this connection it must not be forgotten that while the substantive provisions of a bill may be debated clause by clause, a draft statutory instrument is not subject to any detailed Parliamentary scrutiny. It is either accepted or rejected as a whole. A third is whether the server of the notice may immediately serve another one if the impugned notice is invalid. If he can, that is a pointer towards invalidity."

So, broadly speaking whether or not a s.22 preliminary notice is invalid as a result of some error, omission or other defect will turn on whether Parliament is taken to have intended that such an error etc. invalidated the notice. Of relevance in context is the fact that a tribunal can make an order under s.24 even if the notice fails to comply with the requirements in s.22: see s.24(7)(b) of the 1987 Act. Of greater importance is making sure the notice is error free!

POINTS TO NOTE:

- Check and double check that the circumstances of your application meet the four qualifying criteria for making an application: the tenant critera, the premises criteria, your landlord is not exempt and you have served a s.22 notice or obtained dispensation from that requirement.

- Make sure your preliminary notice is accurate and not missing any information albeit a tribunal has the discretion to make an order even if the notice is deficient in some way or fails to give a reasonable time for remedial action to be taken by the recipient: s.24(7).

- Make sure you document service of the s.22 notice on all recipients – if serving by hand, having a receipt signed off is a useful technique. If serving by post ensure you take advantage of the deemed service provisions under s.7, Interpretation Act 1978.

CHAPTER FOUR

GROUNDS FOR MAKING THE APPLICATION

Once the tenant has served the notice under s.22 of the 1987 Act and time for remedial action in relation to the specified grounds has expired with no or insufficient action on the part of the recipient of that notice (or there was no remedial action capable of being taken in context), it is open to the tenant to apply to the appropriate tribunal for the appointment of a manager.

"The making of a management order is a draconian remedy, which takes away contractual rights and obligations and imposes expense on the parties. Such an order cannot be made unless the statutory conditions are satisfied. Whether an application is based on breaches of obligation by the landlord under s 24(2)(a), or on other circumstances which make it just and convenient to make the appointment under s 24(2)(b), the FTT's power to appoint a manager depends on it being satisfied of the justice and convenience of making an appointment": per Martin Rodger KC in *Invergarry Court Ltd v Connolly* [2022] UKUT 209 (LC) at [55].

The grounds for making such an application are contained in s.24 of the 1987 Act. That section as it currently appears (and there are amendments pending pursuant to the Commonhold and Leasehold Reform Act 2002 and the Freehold and Leasehold Reform Act 2024 which appear below in italics!) deserves setting out in full as it is detailed and comprehensive.

The current grounds of which the tribunal must be satisfied *always* involve consideration of whether it is just and convenient to make the order and otherwise can be summarised as follows:

(1) a breach of any obligation owed to the tenant under his tenancy and relating to the management of the premises in question or any part of them;

(2) unreasonable service charges have been made, or are proposed or likely to be made;

(3) unreasonable variable administration charges or prohibited administration charges have been made, or are proposed or likely to be made;

(4) failure to comply with any relevant provision of a code of practice approved by the Secretary of State under section 87 of the Leasehold Reform, Housing and Urban Development Act 1993 (codes of management practice); and/or

(5) other circumstances exist (which make it just and convenient for the order to be made).

Section 24 provides as follows so far as material to this Chapter (including pending amendments in italics):

> "24 Appointment of manager by a tribunal
>
> (1) The appropriate tribunal may, on an application for an order under this section, by order (whether interlocutory or final) appoint a manager to carry out in relation to any premises to which this Part applies—

(a) such functions in connection with the management of the premises, or

(b) such functions of a receiver,

or both, as the tribunal thinks fit.

(2) The appropriate tribunal may only make an order under this section in the following circumstances, namely—

(a) where the tribunal is satisfied—

(i) that any relevant person either is in breach of any obligation owed by him to the tenant under his tenancy and relating to the management of the premises in question or any part of them or (in the case of an obligation dependent on notice) would be in breach of any such obligation but for the fact that it has not been reasonably practicable for the tenant to give him the appropriate notice, and [...]

(iii) that it is just and convenient to make the order in all the circumstances of the case;

(ab) where the tribunal is satisfied—

(i) that unreasonable service charges have been made, or are proposed or likely to be made, and

(ii) that it is just and convenient to make the order in all the circumstances of the case;

(aba) where the tribunal is satisfied—

(i) that unreasonable variable administration charges or prohibited administration charges have been made, or are proposed or likely to be made, and

(ii) that it is just and convenient to make the order in all the circumstances of the case;

(abb) where the tribunal is satisfied—

(i) that there has been a failure to comply with a duty imposed by or by virtue of section 42 or 42A of this Act, and

(ii) that it is just and convenient to make the order in all the circumstances of the case;

(ac) where the tribunal is satisfied—

(i) that any relevant person has failed to comply with any relevant provision of a code of practice approved by the Secretary of State under section 87 of the Leasehold Reform, Housing and Urban Development Act 1993 (codes of management practice), and

(ii) that it is just and convenient to make the order in all the circumstances of the case; or

(ad) where the tribunal is satisfied—

(i) that any relevant person has breached regulations under section 100(1) of the Leasehold and Freehold Reform Act 2024 (requirement to join redress scheme), and

(ii) that it is just and convenient to make the order in all the circumstances of the case;

(b) where the tribunal is satisfied that other circumstances exist which make it just and convenient for the order to be made.

(2ZA) In this section "relevant person" means a person—

(a) on whom a notice has been served under section 22, or

(b) in the case of whom the requirement to serve a notice under that section has been dispensed with by an order under subsection (3) of that section.

(2ZB) Subsection (2)(a) does not apply in respect of a breach of a building safety obligation by an accountable person for a higher-risk building.

(2ZC) In this section—

"accountable person" has the meaning given in section 72 of the Building Safety Act 2022;

"building safety obligation" means an obligation of an accountable person under Part 4 of the Building Safety Act 2022 or regulations made under that Part;

"higher-risk building" has the meaning given in section 65 of the Building Safety Act 2022.

(2A) For the purposes of subsection (2)(ab) a service charge shall be taken to be unreasonable—

(a) if the amount is unreasonable having regard to the items for which it is payable,

(b) if the items for which it is payable are of an unnecessarily high standard, or

(c) if the items for which it is payable are of an insufficient standard with the result that additional service charges are or may be incurred.

In that provision and this subsection "service charge" means a service charge within the meaning of section 18(1) of the Landlord and Tenant Act 1985, other than one excluded from that section by section 27 of that Act (rent of dwelling registered and not entered as variable).

(2B) In subsection (2)(aba) "variable administration charge" has the meaning given by paragraph 1 of Schedule 11 to the Commonhold and Leasehold Reform Act 2002[, and "prohibited administration charge" means an administration charge which is not payable because of paragraph 2A of that Schedule.

(2C)-(9) […]."

It is apparent from the above that some grounds require breaches by "a relevant person" defined as the person on whom the s.22 notice was served or would have been served but for dispensation, and others do not.

There is significant overlap with the statutory regulation of the leasehold sector in the Landlord and Tenant Act 1985, namely the reasonableness and recoverability of service charges and administration charges. Significant failures to ensure proper management of service and administration charges resulting in excessive costs or poor value for money should be evidenced by applications to the tribunal challenging those charges under ss.27A and 19 of the LTA 1985 and/or Schedule 11 of the CLRA 2002 (and any determinations relied on). Likewise, failures to comply with the RICS Service Charge Residential Management Code might feature in a service charge dispute where the cost of management is challenged as not value for money. Such findings as might have been made should be included as part of an application under s.24.

Whether it is just and convenient to make the order in all the circumstances involves consideration of the case in the round including the nature and severity of the breaches, whether there have been multiple grounds made out, the likelihood of better management by the incumbent without the making of an order, the cost of appointing a manager, the scale of the premises and number of disgruntled tenants and so on.

Building safety concerns

It is important to acknowledge that the ground under subs.(2)(a) relating to breach of an obligation to the tenant by a relevant person is disapplied in respect of a breach of a building safety obligation by an accountable person for a higher-risk building: subs.(2ZA). This is because there is a statutory scheme dealing with such matters under the BSA 2022. Management failings by an accountable person in relation to a higher-risk building are dealt with via the Building Safety Regulator.

A higher-risk building is defined in s.65 of the BSA 2022 as a building in England that (a) is at least 18 metres in height or has at least 7 storeys, and (b) contains at least 2 residential units, meaning a dwelling, or any other unit of living accommodation: s.115, BSA

2022. Regulations made under s.65 have supplemented the definition of higher risk building: see Higher-Risk Buildings (Descriptions and Supplementary Provisions) Regulations 2023, SI 2023/275, regs.7 and 8. Broadly the regulations exclude from the definition certain types of buildings including care homes, secure residential institutions, hotels and accommodation provided by the Ministry of Defence.

For these purposes, "accountable person" is defined by reference to s.72 of the Building Safety Act 2022 which states an accountable person for a higher risk building for leasehold (as opposed to commonhold land) is:

> "(a) a person who holds a legal estate in possession in any part of the common parts (subject to subsection (2)), or
>
> (b) a person who does not hold a legal estate in any part of the building but who is under a relevant repairing obligation in relation to any part of the common parts. [...]
>
> (2) A person ("the estate owner") who holds a legal estate in possession in the common parts of a higher-risk building or any part of them ("the relevant common parts") is not an accountable person for the building by virtue of subsection (1)(a) if—
>
> (a) each long lease of which the estate owner is lessor provides that a particular person, who does not hold a legal estate in any part of the building, is under a relevant repairing obligation in relation to all of the relevant common parts, or
>
> (b) all repairing obligations relating to the relevant common parts which would otherwise be obligations

> of the estate owner are functions of an RTM company."

By s.72(5) of the BSA 2022, where a higher-risk building is on commonhold land, the commonhold association is the accountable person for the building for the purposes of this Part.

Section 72(6) defines "common parts" for the purposes of the above as

> "(a) the structure and exterior of the building, except so far as included in a demise of a single dwelling or of premises to be occupied for the purposes of a business, or (b) any part of the building provided for the use, benefit and enjoyment of the residents of more than one residential unit (whether alone or with other persons)".

A "building safety obligation" is defined by reference to the whole of Part 4 of the BSA 2022 which contains numerous obligations on the part of accountable persons including assessing risks and taking steps to manage and/or remedy them.

For those who consider their case may involve breach of a building safety obligation in relation to a higher risk building, they should take steps to identify whether the circumstances of their case fall within the BSA 2022 as mentioned.

Future grounds

At the time of writing, the amendments to be implemented under the Leasehold and Freehold Reform Act 2024 remain outstanding. Those amendments address the following in summary. There are two new grounds for appointing a manager (also requiring the tribunal to be satisfied it is just and convenient to make an order), namely:

(1) a failure to comply with a duty imposed by or by virtue of section 42 or 42A of the 1987 Act (which impose obligations relating to service charges held on trust for the tenants and ensuring funds are held in designated accounts), and

(2) breach of regulations under section 100(1) of the Leasehold and Freehold Reform Act 2024 (requirement to join redress scheme).

In addition to these extra grounds, the FLRA 2024 will introduce a restriction where a special measures order relating to the building is in force, namely that an order under s.24 may not provide for a manager to carry out a function which the special measures order provides is to be carried out by the special measures manager for the building. Special measures orders and their managers are catered for under the BSA 2022. The introduction of a new s.24A enabling a special measures manager under the BSA 2022 to apply to the tribunal for an order appointing a manager under s.24 is a complementary provision. The grounds for applying will include the tribunal being satisfied that the making of the order is just and equitable and that:

(1) there has been a breach of any obligation owed to the special measures manager by virtue of a special measures order, and

(2) that other circumstances exist which make it just and convenient for the order to be made.

The inclusion of building safety related grounds has led to the introduction of the power to vary or discharge an order of the Tribunal's own motion rather than on the application of an interested (or relevant) person.

POINTS TO NOTE:

- Ensure you set out all available grounds for applying to appoint a manager in the s.22 notice as you may be limited to those grounds only. If you have determinations from the tribunal on service charge or administration charge issues, have them ready to go.
- Check to ensure your circumstances are not excluded under the Building Safety Act 2022.
- Check to see if the new grounds under the Freehold and Leasehold Reform Act 2024 have been appointed (www.legislation.gov.uk will tell you).
- Ensure you document all facts which go to the "just and convenient" test early on in the process because once a ground is made out, the tribunal's focus will shift to the future and the likelihood of the incumbent management improving the position in the future. Make sure your nominated manager is prepped and ready to address the tribunal on all relevant issues.

CHAPTER FIVE

THE TRIBUNAL'S ROLE

This Chapter will consider the process for getting an application in front of the tribunal, the hearing and the management order the tribunal might make.

Can an application to the tribunal be made?

The proposed applicant must be satisfied that they qualify to make an application to the tribunal by reference to the qualification criteria discussed in Chapter 2.

As we have seen in that Chapter, an application is off the cards if a s.22 notice has not been served or dispensation has not been granted or if the recipient of the notice has complied with it within the period specified.

Starting the application

Assuming a green light on making an application, the starting point for a proposed applicant is completing the correct form and becoming familiar with the relevant procedure rules.

The application form for use in England is "Leasehold 2" available from the www.gov.uk website. In Wales, the form is "LVT8" found at www.gov.wales website. Both are broadly similar and require the applicant to set out their details, the property details, the respondent's details, the order sought, the grounds for the application, the nominated manager's details, whether a hearing is needed, an appropriate venue, and whether an order limiting costs is sought.

The form sets out how and where the form is lodged: by email in an attached Microsoft Word document sent to the regional tribunal address listed at the rear of the form. Paper applications are still accepted but will be much slower to process.

A fee is usually payable for the application to be issued by the tribunal (currently £110) unless the tenant qualifies for a waiver. The applicable fees can be found on the form along with details on how to pay – by electronic payment (in which case a tick box must be checked for those details to be provided) or by a cheque accompanying a paper copy of the emailed application and made out to HM Courts and Tribunal Service.

In England, if an application is to be brought in the FTT (the usual starting point), the appropriate rules are The Tribunal Procedure (First-tier Tribunal) (Property Chamber) Rules 2013 (as amended) ("the FTT Procedure Rules") available at https://www.gov.uk/government/publications/property-chamber-tribunal-procedure-rules and in Wales, The Leasehold Valuation Tribunals (Procedure) (Wales) Regulations 2004 available at https://www.legislation.gov.uk/wsi/2004/681/contents/made.

A draft form of management order will need to be provided as part of the application or subsequently in accordance with directions. The nominated manager will need to be asked about what that order should include to best address the management failings and needs going forward. The tribunals have helpfully produced a Practice Statement which sets out in clear terms the tribunals expectations of its appointed managers in terms of qualifications, familiarity with the premises and proposals for handover and future management, and it helpfully includes a draft form of management order. The latest version of the Practice Statement (July 2023) is included at annex 1 of this book and is available online at https://www.judiciary.uk/wp-content/uploads/2022/01/AOM-Practice-Statement-July-2023.pdf.

On receipt of the application, it is for the tribunal to serve it and associated documents on the respondent and any interested parties: r.29(1), FTT Procedure Rules.

Tribunal directions

Usually, the first directions from the tribunal are sent out by email and are sent without there having been a hearing. Those initial directions may list a case management hearing at which the parties will be expected to try and narrow the issues between them and at which directions to a final hearing will be set down.

Directions will ordinarily look to plug any gaps in the application if there are any (such as ensuring the draft management order is in the recommended format and addresses all material issues). They will recommend that the parties try to mediate the dispute first. There will be a direction for a response to the application from the respondent. What follows is usually disclosure of documents supporting the application and response followed by witness statements of the parties and the manager as well as any management plan to be filed and served. This is often accompanied by permission for any expert evidence (e.g., relating to remedial works required to dilapidations at the premises or an accountant if there is alleged financial mismanagement).

The directions then look to list a final hearing on specified dates. For anyone attending a case management hearing, it is important to know likely availability of witnesses and experts as well as who the nominated manager will be in order to avoid the need to adjourn a hearing or, as is more likely, having to attend without the benefit of that witness giving oral evidence (which, because they have not been cross-examined, diminishes the weight to be attached to it).

The final hearing or trial

The tribunal will be initially concerned to ensure that any one of the grounds are made out if disputed, and thereafter that it is just and convenient to make an order in all the circumstances.

Once *one* of the grounds is made out (which may be admitted), that opens a gateway and the hearing before the tribunal will then focus on whether it is "just and convenient" to make an order. When considering what is "just" in this context the tribunal may have regard to the nature and extent of the grounds giving rise to the application but the manager's appointment deals with the future only. Therefore, in considering whether it is just and convenient to make an order, the tribunal will be concerned mainly with the landlord or management company's likely future management (which will be judged to an extent on what has gone before but e.g. a new managing agent may be appointed in advance of the application or hearing to show a willingness to do better in future).

Some consideration of the history of management may be relevant to the issue of the landlord's likely future conduct especially if absenteeism or repair recalcitrance is in issue. But there is a temptation for applicants to become "bogged down" in the historic failures of their landlord and to lose focus on the future management of the premises. Factors that weigh in favour of it being just and convenient to make an order might include a wholesale breakdown in relations between tenants and the landlord, a refusal to appoint new managing agents, an inexperienced landlord, fraudulent or negligent excess charging of service charges. Factors that weigh against the test being satisfied would be the landlord entering into a new managing agent contract for a lengthy period with a reputable firm, a change of freeholder, an inability to do works owing to there being no reserve fund, personal animosity between tenants and the landlord or an RTM Co. which will not be resolved by the appointment of a manager.

Applicants are encouraged not to neglect, whether in the application or in evidence, the "just and convenient test" and to ensure that they address how management efficiencies and cost would improve under the management plan of the nominated manager.

A key point to address is the landlord's response to service of the s.22 notice – has the landlord paid lip-service to the grounds and any remedial works required? Has he ignored it? Has he taken retaliatory action as happened in *Queensbridge Investments v Lodge* [2015] UKUT 635 (LC); [2016] L. & T. R. 19? In that case, the landlord's response to service of the s.22 notice was to pursue the tenants for breach of the subletting covenants in their leases which had been known of for some time.

Nominated manager

Of critical importance will be scrutiny of the nominated manager and that manager's plans for management. As part of that consideration, the tribunal will want to hear from the nominated manager and heavily scrutinse his identity, experience and the management plan proffered. Applicants should ensure their nominated manager is ready to address the factors in the Practice Statement, namely:

(1) Are they a named person and not a company or firm;

(2) Do they understand the manager is to take responsibility for the duties of management albeit they can call on a company or firm to provide them with resources to do so;

(3) There is no conflict of interest in taking up appointment and the manager must seek to avoid conflict of interest in the placing of contracts and discharging their other duties during their appointment. If in doubt about whether a conflict arises, the Manager should seek directions from the Tribunal.

(4) The Manager's understanding that he is appointed as an officer of the Tribunal and must act independently of the parties.

(5) Membership of a professional body at a level of seniority commensurate with the responsibilities of a Tribunal appointed manager;

(6) An understanding of the duties of a Manager set out in the Service Charge Residential Management Code ("the Code") (3rd Edition);

(7) A reasonable period of experience as a manager, an understanding of the RICS code and (if relevant) demonstrable experience of dealing with large scale projects or difficult buildings;

(8) Professional indemnity insurance which is appropriate having regard to the nature of the subject premises and extensive enough to include tasks undertaken during appointment. The PI insurance may be held by the proposed Manager's firm as long as it expressly covers the additional risks/burdens which may affect an appointed Manager;

(9) A complaints procedure in accordance with, or substantially similar to, the requirements of the Royal Institution of Chartered Surveyors;

(10) Membership of a client money protection scheme or an alternative reputable scheme for the same purpose.

(11) Details of any previous Tribunal case under section 24 of the Landlord and Tenant Act 1987 where they were nominated to be the Manager by any party. This information is required whether or not the Tribunal decided to make the appointment as requested. This requirement includes any appointment which is still extant and any appointment which has expired.

(12) Before the substantive hearing the Tribunal expects the proposed manager to have:

   a. Inspected the premises;

   b. Read the Tribunal papers to understand the problems that are required to be addressed;

   c. Familiarised themselves with the leases;

   d. Produced a management plan; and

   e. Read the annexed draft Management Order.

The Practice Statement provides that a management plan should include the following (as relevant):

a. A timetable and plan for handover from the current manager. This should include a list of essential documents such as service charge statements, accounts (audited if required), details of relevant contracts concerning the management of the property, schedules of service charge payments and arrears and budgets which are to be delivered to the Manager;

b. Details of accounts into which service charge funds are to be transferred;

c. Details of a plan to implement all Health and Safety and fire safety measures, including procurement of all relevant records and documentation;

d. Description of resources that will be allocated to management (number and qualifications of staff and time to be spent on property);

e. Description of tasks for day to day running of property;

f. Prioritisation of remedial tasks;

g. Proposals for collection of arrears;

h. Proposals for collection of additional funds (may depend on Tribunal order);

i. Details of professional contacts: lawyers, accountants, surveyors;

j. Proposals for communications with leaseholders and landlord(s);

k. Details of proposed remuneration.

It should not be forgotten that the respondent landlord can propose his own manager as an alternative to that advanced by the applicants. Even then, the tribunal is not bound to accept either nominated candidate and has been known to adjourn for an alternative to be nominated if the tribunal is dissatisfied with those put forward. It is commonly the case that a nominated manager with prior associations to the premises is unlikely to be viewed favourably. It is common for a landlord to put forward a nominated manager who works for the incumbent managing agent for example.

Nominated managers should understand what they are signing themselves up for… relations between landlords, tenants, other tenants, RTM Companies and managing agents may be strained if not entirely broken. A person with grit and good communication skills is an imperative.

The tribunal's order

We looked at s.24(1) to (2D) in Chapter 4. Subsection (1) remains relevant and the remaining subsections of s.24 concern the nature of the order a tribunal can make. They read as follows:

> "(1) The appropriate tribunal may, on an application for an order under this section, by order (whether interlocutory or final) appoint a manager to carry out in relation to any premises to which this Part applies—
>
> (a) such functions in connection with the management of the premises, or
>
> (b) such functions of a receiver,
>
> or both, as the tribunal thinks fit.
>
> […] (2E) An order under this section may not provide for a manager to carry out a function in relation to a higher-risk building where Part 4 of the

Building Safety Act 2022 or regulations made under that Part provide for that function to be carried out by an accountable person for that building.

(3) The premises in respect of which an order is made under this section may, if the tribunal thinks fit, be either more or less extensive than the premises specified in the application on which the order is made.

(4) An order under this section may make provision with respect to—

(a) such matters relating to the exercise by the manager of his functions under the order, and

(b) such incidental or ancillary matters,

as the tribunal thinks fit; and, on any subsequent application made for the purpose by the manager, the tribunal may give him directions with respect to any such matters.

(5) Without prejudice to the generality of subsection (4), an order under this section may provide—

(a) for rights and liabilities arising under contracts to which the manager is not a party to become rights and liabilities of the manager;

(b) for the manager to be entitled to prosecute claims in respect of causes of action (whether contractual or tortious) accruing before or after the date of his appointment;

(c) for remuneration to be paid to the manager by any relevant person, or by the tenants of the premises in respect of which the order is made or by all or any of those persons;

(d) for the manager's functions to be exercisable by him (subject to subsection (9)) either during a specified period or without limit of time.

(6) Any such order may be granted subject to such conditions as the tribunal thinks fit, and in particular its operation may be suspended on terms fixed by the tribunal.

(7) In a case where an application for an order under this section was preceded by the service of a notice under section 22, the tribunal may, if it thinks fit, make such an order notwithstanding—

(a) that any period specified in the notice in pursuance of subsection (2)(d) of that section was not a reasonable period, or

(b) that the notice failed in any other respect to comply with any requirement contained in subsection (2) of that section or in any regulations applying to the notice under section 54(3).

(8) The Land Charges Act 1972 and the Land Registration Act 2002 shall apply in relation to an order made under this section as they apply in relation to an order appointing a receiver or sequestrator of land."

The above is of real significance:

(1) The tribunal can make an order on an "interlocutory" or "final" basis – meaning that an order could be made to address e.g., urgent matters like buildings insurance being placed more quickly than any outstanding but non-urgent matters.

(2) The tribunal can appoint a manager to carry out management or receiver functions in relation to any premises to which this Part applies as the tribunal thinks fit. "Management" of premises is defined in s.24(11) as including references to the repair, maintenance, improvement or insurance of those premises. The functions of a receiver are essentially the ability to "receive" monies which would otherwise be paid to the landlord such as service charges, rents or other rights to receive under contracts for the management of the property. It is important to remember that in *Maunder Taylor v Blaquiere* (above), the tribunal was clear that the manager did not step into the shoes of the landlord and so was unlikely to *be* a receiver in the strict sense (being a receiver would render him liable to sue and be sued), and the wording of s.24(1) is deliberate in referring to the "functions" of a receiver rather than the "status" of a receiver.

(3) The premises in respect of which an order is made may, if the tribunal thinks fit, be either more or less extensive than the premises specified in the application on which the order is made. It could therefore include or exclude associated commercial premises e.g., albeit if the service charge recoverable is apportioned across residential and commercial premises, it will be hard to separate out the commercial premises from management.

(4) An order may make provision with respect to

a. such matters relating to the exercise by the manager of his functions under the order, and

b. such incidental or ancillary matters,

as the tribunal thinks fit; and, on any subsequent application made for the purpose by the manager, the tribunal may give him directions with respect to any such matters.

(5) An order may provide

a. for rights and liabilities arising under contracts to which the manager is not a party to become rights and liabilities of the manager (which removes scope for contractual disputes arising from the appointment such as a refusal to engage or an attempt to renegotiate for a higher price and allows the manager to bring contracts to an end where appropriate);

b. for the manager to be entitled to prosecute claims in respect of causes of action (whether contractual or tortious) accruing before or after the date of his appointment;

c. for remuneration to be paid to the manager by any relevant person, or by the tenants of the premises in respect of which the order is made or by all or any of those persons;

d. for the manager's functions to be exercisable by him either during a specified period or without limit of time (save that such an order can be discharged or varied at any time under s.24(9)). This would e.g., allow an order to terminate on the occurring of an event such as the sale of the freehold reversion of leases to a third party. There is an attractiveness to having an order without limit of time but this is rarely seen to be just and convenient and so a long-stop is the preferred option. That said, if an extension of that period is needed it should be applied for long before the expiry of the management order otherwise the order lapses and the process must start again. An extension of the order does not require the court to be satisfied of the s.24 criteria again: see the Court of Appeal decision in *Orchard Court Residents Association v St Anthony's Homes Ltd* [2003] EWCA Civ 1049; [2003] 2 E.G.L.R. 28.

(6) An order may not provide for a manager to carry out a function in relation to a higher-risk building where Part 4 of the Building Safety Act 2022 or regulations made under that Part provide for that function to be carried out by an accountable person for that building.

(7) An order may be granted subject to such conditions as the tribunal thinks fit, and in particular its operation may be suspended on terms fixed by the tribunal. This might be used where an application for the right to manage has also been made or where a landlord undertakes to appoint a new managing agent.

(8) The order must be registered against the landlord's title under the Land Charges Act 1972 and the Land Registration Act 2002. Under s.87, Land Registration Act 2002, the form of registration and therefore of protecting an order appointing a receiver or sequestrator (and by extension a management order) is by the entry of a restriction: see *Urwick v Pickard* [2019] UKUT 365 (LC); [2020] L. & T.R. 9. at [36].

The Practice Statement contains a template form of order which contemplates issues arising under all of the above headings. It is absolutely crucial for the applicant to include everything they need or might want in the terms of the order sought because the source of the manager's powers and duties is the order itself. Whilst the parties or manager can come back for a direction from the tribunal or a variation or discharge of the terms or any one of them of the order, this will incur additional costs and time.

Finally, it is important to remember that the manager is an officer of the tribunal and is not the agent of the tenants appointing him. This is illustrated in *Maunder Taylor v Blaquiere* (above) itself where the litigation was precipitated by Mr Maunder Taylor suing a tenant who had appointed him for arrears of service charges.

So what happens to the lease terms once an order is made? In *Chuan-Hui v K Group Holdings Inc.* [2021] EWCA Civ 403, the Court of Appeal per Henderson LJ held (at [56]):

> The Upper Tribunal was in my view substantially correct to say, at [53]:
>
> 'The imposition of a management order does not displace the lease covenants and the lessees remain bound by them.'
>
> This sentence must, however, be read subject to the proviso that it refers to the underlying contractual framework, which remains in place subject to the terms of the management order. Plainly, to the extent that the terms of the order are in conflict with the underlying contract, the former must prevail while the order remains in force."

Ensuring that what is wanted and needed from a management perspective is included in the order is important but so is ensuring that the manager does not inadvertently become responsible for matters he has no business managing such as lease assignments, granting licences for structural alterations, assuming personal liability for compliance with the landlord's covenants and so on. These types of rights and obligations go to the very ownership of the freehold reversion which remains vested in the landlord and places a manager in a difficult and undesirable position.

Costs

In the context of an application for the appointment of a manager under s.24 of the 1987 Act the tribunal rules on costs appear at rule 13 of the FTT Procedure Rules in England. There is no equivalent in the Welsh LVT Procedure Rules. They provide that the tribunal may make an order in respect of costs *only*:

(1) under s.29(4) of the Tribunals Courts and Enforcement Act 2007 (wasted costs) and the costs incurred in applying for such costs; or

(2) if a person has acted unreasonably in bringing, defending or conducting proceedings.

The general rule is therefore that an applicant cannot recover their costs from the other side in the FTT and *vice versa*. This general rule is subject to the above and the threshold of conduct is high.

"Wasted costs" is a term of art and defined in s.29(5) of the 2007 Act as:

> "any costs incurred by a party—

> (a) as a result of any improper, unreasonable or negligent act or omission on the part of any legal or other representative or any employee of such a representative, or
>
> (b) which, in the light of any such act or omission occurring after they were incurred, the relevant Tribunal considers it is unreasonable to expect that party to pay.
>
> (6) In this section "legal or other representative", in relation to a party to proceedings, means any person exercising a right of audience or right to conduct the proceedings on his behalf."

More commonly encountered in practice is the argument that a party has engaged in "unreasonable behaviour". This includes conduct which is "vexatious" and "designed to harass the other side... the acid test is whether the conduct permits of a reasonable explanation...": see *Ridehalgh v Horsefield* [1994] Ch 205; *Willow Court Man. Co. v Alexander* [2016] UKUT 290 (LC); and *Lea (and other leaseholders) v GP Ilfracombe Management Company Ltd* [2024] EWCA Civ 1241, [2025] 1 WLR 371, in which the Court of Appeal applied *Willow* and *Ridehalgh* and held that the proper approach involves three stages:

> "28. At the first stage the question is whether a person has acted unreasonably. A decision that the conduct of a party has been unreasonable does not involve an exercise of discretion but rather the application of an objective standard of conduct to the facts of the case. If there is no reasonable explanation for the conduct complained of, the behaviour will properly be adjudged to be unreasonable, and the threshold for the making of

> an order will have been crossed. A discretionary power is then engaged and the decision maker moves to a second stage of the inquiry. At that second stage it is essential for the tribunal to consider whether, in the light of the unreasonable conduct it has found to have been demonstrated, it ought to make an order for costs or not; it is only if it decides that it should make an order that a third stage is reached when the question is what the terms of that order should be."

In *Staples v Cranfield* [2018] UKUT 341 (LC) the FTT made a costs order for unreasonable conduct in the context of an application for the variation of a management order. On appeal to the UT, it was argued that the FTT had no jurisdiction to make such an order because the application to vary the order was not defending or conducting proceedings. HHJ Huskinson disagreed, finding that the application to vary formed part of the previous proceedings for the appointment of a manager.

Protection from costs of relevant person: s.20C

Applicants should scrutinise their leases carefully to see if they contain or may contain a provision that permits the landlord or management company to recover costs of legal proceedings relating to the management of the premises. If there is a risk that this is the case, the applicants should apply for an order under s.20C of the Landlord and Tenant Act 1985 restricting a landlord or management company's ability to recover those costs via the service charge.

Appeal rights

In the event the tribunal makes an order appointing a manager or not, the parties have rights of appeal to the Upper Tribunal (Lands Chamber) conferred by either the Tribunals, Courts and Enforcement Act 2007 s.11 (on a point of law) or the Commonhold and Leasehold Reform Act 2002 s.176B (on any ground other than a point of law insofar as it relates to a question under inter alia the Landlord and Tenant Act 1987).

Permission to appeal must be sought from the FTT first within 28 days of the reasons for the decision being sent out and, if refused, may be sought from the Upper Tribunal within a further 14 days of notification of the FTT's refusal. If the Upper Tribunal refuses permission to appeal, the appellant can apply for judicial review of that decision.

POINTS TO NOTE:

- Do not apply if the remedial action required by the s.22 notice has been complied with fully and in time.

- Understand that once a gateway ground is made out, the tribunal's focus will be on the future and applicants will need to be ready to show why things are unlikely to improve which may be difficult if, e.g., new managing agents are installed in response to the s.22 notice.

- Make sure you are familiar with the Practice Statement annexed to this book.

- Ensure your nominated manager has provided all information referred to in the Practice Statement as well as any additional matters to the tribunal in the form of a witness statement and management plan.

- Be familiar with the FTT Procedure Rules or LVT Procedure Rules as appropriate.

- Know your costs and appeal rights and ensure you apply for costs protection under s.20C where necessary.

CHAPTER SIX

WHAT HAPPENS IF IT GOES WRONG?

You have obtained tribunal determinations of unreasonable service charges, prepared your application for the appointment of a manager, prepped your nominated manager, negotiated with the landlord and appeared at a final hearing, all at substantial cost.

And nothing changes... paying for major works remains a problem because it became apparent on transfer that there was no money in the reserves and leaseholders are unwilling to front load expenditure above and beyond what is permitted by way of actual expenditure under the terms of the lease.

What happens next? Well, better service charge provisions are needed than those contained in the lease which only allow recovery of actual expenditure and, luckily the management order can give the manager the ability to collect on account service charges if he can show it is just and convenient to have it. Remember, his powers are derived from the order which operates in priority to the lease terms. He has no obligation to act in the interest of tenants or the landlord and so any objection to the approach advocated would not prevent the manager taking appropriate action.

The current order did not anticipate this problem as issues with the reserve were not appreciated before the handover. So, a variation of the order is now needed.

Variation

By s.24(9) of the 1987 Act:

> "(9) The appropriate tribunal may, on the application of any person interested, vary or discharge (whether conditionally or unconditionally) an order made under this section; and if the order has been protected by an entry registered under the Land Charges Act 1972 or the Land Registration Act 2002, the tribunal may by order direct that the entry shall be cancelled.
>
> (9A) The tribunal shall not vary or discharge an order under subsection (9) on the application of a relevant person unless it is satisfied—
>
> (a) that the variation or discharge of the order will not result in a recurrence of the circumstances which led to the order being made, and
>
> (b) that it is just and convenient in all the circumstances of the case to vary or discharge the order."

The application can be made by "any person interested" which would include a tenant, landlord or manager as well as anyone affected by the management order such as a mortgagor or the personal representatives of a deceased manager.

Under the amendments in the Freehold and Leasehold Reform Act 2024 (yet to be appointed), the power to vary or discharge will be capable of being exercised of the tribunal's own motion and the reference to an application for variation or discharge by a relevant person will be removed accordingly.

It should be noted that where the application to vary is made by a "relevant person" (remember s.24(2ZA), which defines this as a person who receives the s.22 notice or in respect of which such a notice would have been served if dispensation had not been granted) any application by that person is subject to a higher test for the variation, namely that the variation will not result in a recurrence of the circumstances which led to the order being made, and that it is just and convenient in all the circumstances of the case to vary the order.

No such limitation applies to consideration of whether to vary the order for any other applicant albeit it is likely that a tribunal will consider whether it is just and convenient for the variation to be made.

Discharge

The above applies equally in the context of an application to discharge an order. This might be sought if e.g., a manager retires or considers they cannot effectively manage the block owing to difficulties with the landlord and/or tenants.

It is important to understand that the effect of discharge of the order is that management reverts back to the landlord or management company and the process will have to start all over again with a s.22 notice if a further order is needed.

In the recent decision of *Kirk v Sheffield Bath Company Ltd* [2025] UKUT 111 (LC), the UT held that where an order appointing a manager expired after an application to extend its duration and vary its terms had been made but before the FTT had determined that application, it was wrong to dismiss the application for want of jurisdiction. Martin Rodger KC held at [33] that there was nothing in the language or structure of Part 2 of the 1987 Act, nor any practical consideration, which ruled out treating an application to extend (and vary) the appointment of a manager made before the period of the appointment has expired like any other application for a variation. The President continued at [36], that the fact the manager's appointment has expired without an application being made in sufficient time to enable its orderly consideration, while not fatal, is a matter which can properly be taken into account when considering whether it is just and convenient to order the variation.

An order appointing a manager shall not be discharged by reason only that under s.21(3) (discussed in Chapter 2, above) the premises in respect of which the order was made have ceased to be premises to which this Part applies: s.24(10) of the 1987 Act.

Management Directions

Where a judgment call needs to be made within the terms of the order, relating to the selection of a contractor e.g., or the appropriate method of conducting remedial works, s.24(4) of the 1987 Act permits the manager (and only the manager) to make an application to the tribunal for directions to be given with respect to the exercise of his functions.

Enforcement of the order

An order of the tribunal in England that is not for the payment of money is enforceable under the Commonhold and Leasehold Reform Act 2002, s.176C and the Civil Procedure Rules ("CPR") Part 70. An equivalent enforcement provision to s.176C of the 2002 Act appears in rule 19 of the Welsh LVT Procedure Rules.

Section 176C provides:

> "Any decision of the First-tier Tribunal or Upper Tribunal under or in connection with an enactment specified in section 176A(2), other than a decision ordering the payment of a sum (as to which see section 27 (enforcement) of the Tribunals, Courts and Enforcement Act 2007), is to be enforceable with the permission of a county court in the same way as orders of such a court."

The enforcement of a management order can therefore be achieved by either:

(1) The making of an application to the tribunal under the Landlord and Tenant Act 1987 s.24(4) for the attachment of a penal notice to the order, or to those provision(s) of it that require enforcement. This approach was approved in *Coates v Octagon Overseas Ltd, Canary Riverside Estate Management Ltd* [2017] EWHC 877 (Ch); [2017] 4W.L.R. 91 *per* Judge Karen Walden-Smith at [35], where she was clear that applying to the County Court for an injunction which had the effect of enlarging the scope of the management order was outside the County Court's jurisdiction and wholly inappropriate. Whilst this may be thought only to apply to a recalcitrant landlord or tenant, it might equally apply to a wayward tribunal appointed manager as can be demonstrated by *Maharaj & Lo Porto v Richard Davidoff (Tribunal appointed manager)* LON/00AL/LSC/2020/0111 where the manager charged for items not included in the order, delegated at inflated rates to a managing agent, proceeded with a more expansive specification of works than the management order specified, and paid sums out of the reserve fund to the landlord and other person in breach of fiduciary duty.

(2) The manager may apply to County Court under CPR Part 70 and CPR Practice Direction 70 for permission to enforce the order "in the same way as orders of such a court" pursuant to the2002 Act, s.176C, or under rule 19 of the Welsh LVT Procedure Rules: see *Coates* (above) at [37]. CPR 70 and its accompanying practice direction govern the various ways in which orders can be enforced.

POINTS TO NOTE:

- It can and does go wrong. Expect the unexpected and take early action to remedy any issues where possible.

- Build up your evidence of resistance from those affected by the management order as this will be needed in the event enforcement action is required.

- Beware the effect of discharging a management order. Variation, extension and enforcement are preferable routes to handle ongoing problematic management.

CHAPER SEVEN

CONCLUSION

I sincerely hope that you have derived some use from this book and my attempt to set out in a user-friendly and succinct manner the complexities of this area of residential landlord and tenant law. The area is not straightforward, and I encourage you to read around the subject especially by familiarising yourself with decisions in the FTT on the appointment of managers. There is no substitute to seeing how the tribunal treats different cases according to their facts. Furthermore, the tribunal holds its hearings in public and seeing an appointment of a manager case would be invaluable to anyone embarking on the procedure.

As you will have seen from the previous chapters, there are amendments pending to this area and I encourage anyone reading this book to make sure they check the relevant provisions of the legislation where those amendments are anticipated in the near future under the Freehold and Leasehold Reform Act 2024.

Finally, as with any area of leasehold law in the tribunal, be prepared for every eventuality and take nothing for granted!

APPENDIX A

APPOINTMENT OF MANAGERS UNDER SECTION 24 OF THE LANDLORD AND TENANT ACT 1987

PRACTICE STATEMENT ON THE TRIBUNAL'S CONSIDERATION OF WHO TO APPOINT AS A MANAGER – REVISED VERSION JULY 2023

Introduction

1. The purpose of the statement is to give leaseholders, prospective Managers, and landlords, an indication of the Tribunal's expectations of a proposed Manager when deciding whether to make an order under section 24 of the Landlord and Tenant Act 1987.

2. The power to appoint a manager under Part II of the 1987 Act is a power which will be exercised by a Tribunal in order to resolve a problem in the management of a property. This will either be because the Tribunal is satisfied that any of the specific circumstances under section 24(2) of the Act apply and that it is just and convenient to make the order or that in accordance with section 24(2)(b) that other circumstances exist which make it just and convenient for the order to be made.

3. Amongst other considerations it will not be just and convenient for an order appointing a Manager to be made unless the Tribunal is satisfied that the proposed Manager is suitable. The purpose of this practice statement is to give guidance about the characteristics of a Manager that a Tribunal will wish to be satisfied of before appointing. Because the circumstances of each case differs from another, the status of this document is intended to be as guidance rather than a definitive list of Tribunal requirements. However, the Tribunal will have regard to this statement when reaching their determination.

Identifying a Manager

4. It is for the parties to identify the person that they will ask the Tribunal to appoint as a Manager. That person should usually be identified before a section 24 application is made to the Tribunal.

5. The Tribunal will usually appoint a named person as a Manager rather than a company or a firm. The Tribunal expects the named person to take responsibility for the appointed Manager's duties. The named person may use the resources of their company/firm and receive support from others but the Manager will have ultimate responsibility.

6. Before appointing a person as a Manager, the Tribunal will need to be satisfied that the Manager would have no conflict of interest in taking up appointment. The

Manager must also seek to avoid conflict of interest in the placing of contracts and discharging their other duties during their appointment. A conflict will occur if the dealings would be regarded by the average consumer as conflicting with the Manager's obligations under the order. If in doubt the Manager should seek directions from the Tribunal.

7. A Manager is appointed as an officer of the Tribunal and must act independently of the parties.

8. Save in exceptional circumstances, the Tribunal will not usually appoint a leaseholder as the Manager.

Tribunal Requirements

9. The Tribunal will usually require a proposed Manager to show the following prior to appointment:

    (a) Membership of a professional body at a level of seniority commensurate with the responsibilities of a Tribunal appointed manager;
    (b) An understanding of the duties of a Manager set out in the Service Charge Residential Management Code ("the Code") (3rd Edition);
    (c) A reasonable period of experience as a manager, an understanding of the RICS code and (if relevant) demonstrable experience of dealing with large scale projects or difficult buildings;
    (d) Professional indemnity insurance which is appropriate having regard to the nature of the subject premises and extensive enough to include tasks undertaken during appointment. The PI insurance may be held by the proposed Manager's firm as long as it expressly covers the additional risks/burdens which may affect an appointed Manager;
    (e) A complaints procedure in accordance with, or substantially similar to, the requirements of the Royal Institution of Chartered Surveyors;
    (f) Membership of a client money protection scheme or an alternative reputable scheme for the same purpose.

10. Before the substantive hearing the Tribunal expects the proposed manager to have:
    (a) Inspected the premises;
    (b) Read the Tribunal papers to understand the problems that are required to be addressed;
    (c) Familiarised themselves with the leases;
    (d) Produced a management plan (see below); and
    (e) Have read the annexed draft Management Order.

11. A management plan should include the following (as relevant):

(a) A timetable and plan for handover from the current manager. This should include a list of essential documents such as service charge statements, accounts (audited if required), details of relevant contracts concerning the management of the property, schedules of service charge payments and arrears and budgets which are to be delivered to the Manager;
(b) Details of accounts into which service charge funds are to be transferred;
(c) Details of a plan to implement all Health and Safety and fire safety measures, including procurement of all relevant records and documentation;
(d) Description of resource that will be allocated to management (number and qualifications of staff and time to be spent on property);
(e) Description of tasks for day to day running of property;
(f) Prioritisation of remedial tasks;
(g) Proposals for collection of arrears;
(h) Proposals for collection of additional funds (may depend on Tribunal order);
(i) Details of professional contacts: lawyers, accountants, surveyors;
(j) Proposals for communications with leaseholders and landlord(s);
(k) Details of proposed remuneration.

12. The Manager must provide details of any previous Tribunal case under section 24 of the Landlord and Tenant Act 1987 where they were nominated to be the Manager by any party. This information is required whether or not the Tribunal decided to make the appointment as requested. This requirement includes any appointment which is still extant and any appointment which has expired

Draft Management Order

13. Annexed to this Practice Statement is a **draft** Management Order which the Tribunal will use as the basis for its order if a section 24 application is successful. The Tribunal will adapt the Order in accordance with the circumstances of the case.

14. The parties and the Manager are required to consider the draft order and to provide the Tribunal with their observations and any proposed amendments on the terms of the draft order in good time for the final order to be produced. The Manager should have the ability to carry out all of the obligations set out in the final Order

Siobhan McGrath

President

July 2023

FIRST-TIER TRIBUNAL
PROPERTY CHAMBER (RESIDENTIAL PROPERTY)

Case Reference :

Property :

Applicants :

Representative :

Respondent :

Representative :

The Manager :

Tribunal members :

Date of Order :

MANAGEMENT ORDER

Note to Drafter: Matters identified in square brackets are options to be considered in the context of the specific application before you

Interpretation

1. In this Order:

"The Property" means the flats and other premises known as known as ....and registered at HM Land Registry under title number **[..................]** and shall include [the building, outhouses, gardens, amenity space, drives, pathways landscaped areas, flower beds, passages, bin-stores, common parts, storage rooms basements, electricity and power rooms; and all other parts of the property].

"The Landlord" shall mean [...........] or their successors in title to the reversion immediately expectant upon the Leases.

"The Tenants" shall mean the proprietors for the time being of the Leases whether as lessee or under-lessee and "Tenant" shall be construed accordingly.

"The Leases" shall mean all leases and/or underleases of flats in the Property.

"The Manager" means [...................]

"The Tribunal" means the First-tier Tribunal (Property Chamber)

ORDER

2. In accordance with section 24(1) of the Landlord and Tenant Act 1987 ("the Act") **[** .... Of [firm]**]** is appointed as Manager of the Property.

3. The Manager's appointment shall start on **[**.............**]** ("the start date") and shall end on **[**.............**]** ("the end date"). *NB: good practice might be for the end date to coincide with the end of the service charge year*

4. For the avoidance of doubt this Order supplements but does not displace covenants under the Leases and the Tenants remain bound by them. Where there is a conflict between the provisions of the Order and the Leases, the provisions of the Order take precedence.

5. The purpose of this Management Order is to provide for the management of the Property [which includes taking steps to resolve the following problems of inadequate management identified by the tribunal:]

(a) [...............] *Identify any specific problems*

6. [To address the steps identified in the previous paragraph the Manager is empowered to:

   (a) [...............] *Include here power to take steps that go beyond routine management e.g. provision for the Manager to collect in monies to carry out improvement works, or for the Landlord to contribute towards the costs of repairs*

7. The Manager shall manage the Property in accordance with:

   (a) the terms of this Order and the Directions set out below;

   (b) the respective obligations of the Landlord and the Tenants under the Leases whereby the Property is demised by the Landlord (save where modified by this Order);

   (c) the duties of a Manager set out in the Service Charge Residential Management Code ("the Code") (3rd Edition) or such other replacement code published by the Royal Institution of Chartered Surveyors ("RICS") and approved by the Secretary of State pursuant to section 87 Leasehold Reform Housing and Urban Development Act 1993(whether the Manager is a Member of the RICS or not; and

   (d) the provisions of sections 18 to 30 of the Landlord and Tenant Act 1985.

8. From the date this Order comes into effect, no other party shall be entitled to exercise a management function in respect of the Property where the same is the responsibility of the Manager under this Order.

9. The tribunal requires the Manager to act fairly and impartially in the performance of their functions under this Order and with the skill, care and diligence to be reasonably expected of a Manager experienced in carrying out work of a similar scope and complexity to that required for the performance of the said functions.

10. The Manager or any other interested person may apply to vary or discharge this Order pursuant to the provisions of section 24(9) of the Act.

11. The Tribunal may, upon receipt of information or notification of change of circumstances, issue directions to the parties, or any other interested person, concerning the operation of this Order, both during its term, and after its expiry.

12. Any application to extend or renew this Order **must** be made before the end date, preferably at least three months before that date, and supported by a brief report of the management of the Property during the period of the appointment. Where an application for an extension or renewal is made prior to the end date, then the Manager's appointment will continue until that application has been finally determined.

13. The Manager is appointed to take all decisions about the management of the Property necessary to achieve the purposes of this Order. If the Manager is unable to decide what course to take, the Manager may apply to the Tribunal for further directions, in

accordance with section 24(4), Landlord and Tenant Act 1987. Circumstances in which a request for such directions may be appropriate include, but are not limited to:

(a) a serious or persistent failure by any party to comply with an obligation imposed by this Order;

(b) circumstances where there are insufficient sums held by the Manager to discharge their obligations under this Order and/or for the parties to pay the Manager's remuneration; and

(c) where the Manager is in doubt as to the proper construction and meaning of this Order.

Contracts

14. Rights and liabilities arising under contracts, including any contract of insurance and/or any contract for the provision of any services to the Property, to which the Manager is not a party, but which are relevant to the management of the Property, shall upon the date of appointment become rights and liabilities of the Manager, save that:

(a) the Landlord shall indemnify the Manager for any liabilities arising before commencement of this Order; and

(b) the Manager has the right to decide, in their absolute discretion, the contracts in respect of which they will assume such rights and liabilities, with such decision to be communicated in writing to the relevant parties within 56 days from the date this order.

15. The Manager may place, supervise and administer contracts and check demands for payment of goods, services and equipment supplied for the benefit of the Property.

[Licences to assign, approvals and pre-contract enquiries]

16. [The Manager shall be responsible for carrying out those functions in the residential Leases concerning approvals and permissions, including those for sublettings, assignments, alterations and improvements, that the Leases provide should be carried out by the Landlord.] ***NB:*** *Do NOT include licences to assign and/or approvals unless there is agreement between the parties, or some other exceptional reason as these are Landlord proprietary rights*

17. The Manager shall be responsible for responding to pre-contract enquiries regarding the sale of a residential flat at the Property.

Legal Proceedings

18. The Manager may bring or defend any court or tribunal proceedings relating to management of the Property (whether contractual or tortious) and, subject to the approval of the Tribunal, may continue to bring or defend proceedings relating to the appointment , after the end of their appointment.

19. Such entitlement includes bringing proceedings in respect of arrears of service charge [and rent] attributable to any of the Flats in the Property, including, where appropriate, proceedings before this tribunal under section 27A of the Landlord and Tenant Act 1985 and in respect of administration charges under schedule 11 of the Commonhold and Leasehold Reform Act 2002 or under section 168(4) of that Act or before the courts and shall further include any appeal against any decision made in any such proceedings.

20. The Manager may instruct solicitors, counsel, and other professionals in seeking to bring or defend legal proceedings and is entitled to be reimbursed from the service charge account in respect of costs, disbursements or VAT reasonably incurred in doing so during, or after, this appointment. If costs paid from the service charge are subsequently recovered from another party, those costs must be refunded to the service charge account.

Remuneration

21. [The Tenants are responsible for payment of [..... %] of the Managers' fees, which are to payable under the provisions of this Order but which may be collected under the service charge mechanisms of their Leases][and the Landlord is responsible for payment of [....... %] of those fees] *NB: This allows for a contribution by the Landlord, if appropriate, but must be discussed with the parties*

OR

22. [The Landlord is responsible for payment of the Managers' fees which are to be collected, in the first instance, from the Tenants under the service charge mechanisms of their Leases]. *NB: Use this where the Landlord should be responsible for paying **all** of the Manager's fees but, discuss with the parties before making such provision*

23. The sums payable are:

    (a) an annual fee of [........] per flat for performing the duties set out in paragraph 3.4 of the RICS Code (so far as applicable);

    (b) any additional fees contained in a schedule to this Order for the duties set out in paragraph 3.5 of the RICS Code (so far as applicable); and

    (c) VAT on the above fees.

Ground Rent and Service charge

24. The Manager [shall/shall not] collect the ground rents payable under the residential Leases.

25. The Manager shall collect all service charges and insurance premium contributions payable under the Leases, in accordance with the terms and mechanisms in the Leases.

26. *If appropriate*: Whether or not the terms of any Lease so provides, the Manager shall have the authority to:

(a) demand payments in advance and balancing payments at the end of the accounting year;

(b) establish a sinking fund to meet the Landlord's obligations under the Leases;

(c) allocate credits of service charge due to Tenants at the end of the accounting year to the sinking fund;

(d) alter the accounting year and to collect arrears of service charge and insurance that have accrued before their appointment; and

(e) [............ ....] *Insert any other powers considered necessary*

27. The Manager may set, demand and collect a reasonable service charge to be paid by the Landlord (as if he were a lessee), in respect of any unused premises in part of the Property retained by the Landlord, or let on terms which do not require the payment of a service charge.

If appropriate:

28. [To ensure that the Manager has adequate funds to manage the Property, the Manager may immediately collect £ [...........] from each Tenant and, as the case may be, [£.......] from the Landlord. Any sum demanded by the Manager shall be payable within 28 days.]

29. The Manager is entitled to recover through the service charge the reasonable cost and fees of any surveyors, architects, solicitors, counsel, and other professional persons or firms, incurred by them whilst carrying out their functions under the Order.

Administration Charges

30. The Manager may recover administration charges from individual Tenants for their costs incurred in collecting ground rent, service charges and insurance which includes the costs of reminder letters, transfer of files to solicitors and letters before action. Such charges will be subject to legal requirements as set out in schedule 11 of the Commonhold and Leasehold Reform Act 2002. The Details of the fees charged are set out in the Appendix of additional fees.

Disputes

31. In the event of a dispute regarding the payability of any sum payable under this Order by the lessees, additional to those under the Leases (including as to the remuneration payable to the Manager and litigation costs incurred by the Manager), a Tenant, or the Manager, may apply to the tribunal seeking a determination under section 27A of the Landlord and Tenant Act 1985 as to whether the sum in dispute is payable and, if so, in what amount.

32. In the event of a dispute regarding the payability of any sum payable under this Order by the landlord, other than a payment under a Lease, the Manager or the Landlord may

apply to the tribunal seeking a determination as to whether the sum in dispute is payable and, if so, in what amount.

33. In the event of dispute regarding the conduct of the management of the property by the Manager, any person interested may apply to the Tribunal to vary or discharge the order in accordance with section 24(9) of the Landlord and Tenant Act 1987.

34. In the event of a dispute regarding the reimbursement of unexpended monies at the end of the Manager's appointment, the Manager, a Tenant, or the Landlord may apply to the Tribunal for a determination as to what monies, if any, are payable, to whom, and in what amount.

DIRECTIONS TO LANDLORD

35. The Landlord must comply with the terms of this Order.

36. On any disposition [other than a charge] of the Landlord's estate in the Property, the Landlord will procure from the person to whom the Property is to be conveyed, a direct covenant with the Manager, that the said person will (a) comply with the terms of this Order; and (b) on any future disposition (other than a charge) procure a direct covenant in the same terms from the person to whom the Property is to be conveyed.
37. The Landlord shall give all reasonable assistance and co-operation to the Manager in pursuance of their functions, rights, duties and powers under this Order, and shall not interfere or attempt to interfere with the exercise of any of the Manager's said rights, duties or powers except by due process of law.
38. The Landlord is to allow the Manager and their employees and agents access to all parts of the Property and must provide keys, passwords, and any other documents or information necessary for the practical management of the Property in order that the Manager might conveniently perform their functions and duties, and exercise their powers under this Order.
39. Within [x] days from the date of this Order the Landlord must provide all necessary information to the Manager to provide for an orderly transfer of responsibilities, to include the transfer of:

    (a) all accounts, books and records relating to the Property, including a complete record of all unpaid service charges; and

    (b) all funds relating to the Property including uncommitted service charges and any monies standing to the credit of a reserve or sinking fund.

DIRECTIONS TO MANAGER

40. The Manager must adhere to the terms of the Order above.

Entry of a Form L restriction in the Register of the Landlord's Registered Estate

41. To protect the direction in paragraph 36 for procurement by the Landlord, of a direct covenant with the Manager, **the Manager must apply** for the entry of the following restriction in the register of the Landlord's estate under title no(s) [.........................].

"No disposition of the registered estate (other than a charge) by the proprietor of the registered estate, or by the proprietor of any registered charge, not being a charge registered before the entry of this restriction, is to be completed by registration without a certificate signed by the applicant for registration [or their conveyancer] that the provisions of paragraph 36 of an Order of the Tribunal dated [.................] have been complied with" *[Careful cross-check of the paragraph numbering of the Directions to the Landlord above is essential]*

Registration

The Manager must make an application to HM Land Registry for entry of the restriction referred to in paragraph 41, within 14 days of the date of this Order. *[Careful cross-check of the paragraph numbering of the Directions to the Manager above is essential]*

42. A copy of the Order should accompany the application (unless it is submitted by a solicitor able to make the necessary declaration at Box 8(c) of the RX1 application form). The application should confirm that:

- this is an Order made under the Landlord and Tenant Act 1987, Part II (Appointment of Managers by a Tribunal) and that pursuant to section 24(8) of the 1987 Act, the Land Registration Act 2002 shall apply in relation to an Order made under this section as they apply in relation to an order appointing a receiver or sequestrator of land.
- Consequently, pursuant to Rule 93(s) of the Land Registration Rules 2003, the Manager is a person regarded as having sufficient interest to apply for a restriction in standard Form L or N.

Conflicts of Interest

43. The Manager must be astute to avoid any Conflict of Interest between their duties and obligations under this Order, and their contractual dealings. Where in doubt, the Manager should apply to the Tribunal for directions.

Complaints

44. The Manager must operate a complaints procedure in accordance with, or substantially similar to, the requirements of the Royal Institution of Chartered Surveyors.

Insurance

45. The Manager must maintain appropriate building insurance for the Property and ensure that the Manager's interest is noted on the insurance policy.

46. From the date of appointment, and throughout the appointment, the Manager must ensure that he/she has appropriate professional indemnity insurance cover in the sum of at least £2 million [or £ x million] and shall provide copies of the certificate of liability insurance to the Tribunal, and, upon request, to any Tenant or the Landlord. The Certificate should specifically state that it applies to the duties of a Tribunal appointed Manager.

Accounts

47. The Manager must:

(a) prepare and submit to the Landlord and the Tenants an annual statement of account detailing all monies receivable, received and expended. The accounts are to be certified by the external auditor, if required under the Leases;

(b) maintain efficient records and books of account and to produce for these for inspection, to include receipts or other evidence of expenditure, upon request by the Landlord or a Tenant under section 22 Landlord and Tenant Act 1985;

(c) maintain on trust in an interest-bearing account at such bank or building society, as the Manager shall from time to time decide, into which ground rent, service charge contributions, Insurance Rent, and all other monies arising under the Leases shall be paid; and

(d) hold all monies collected in accordance with the provisions of the Code.

Repairs and maintenance

48. The Manager must:

(a) by [..........] draw up a planned maintenance programme for the period of the appointment, allowing for the periodic re-decoration and repair of the exterior and interior common parts of the Property, as well as any roads, accessways, mechanical, electrical and other installations serving the Property, and shall send a copy to every Tenant and to the Landlord;

(b) subject to receiving sufficient prior funds:

(i) carry out all required repair and maintenance required at the Property, in accordance with the Landlord's covenants in the Leases, including instructing contractors to attend and rectify problems, and is entitled to recover the cost of doing so as service charge payable under the Leases or in accordance with the Order.

(ii) arrange and supervise any required major works to the Property, including preparing a specification of works and obtaining competitive tenders.

(c) liaise with all relevant statutory bodies in the carrying out of their management functions under the Order; and

(d) ensure that the Landlord, and the Tenants, are consulted on any planned and major works to the Property and to give proper regard to their views.

49. The Manager has the power to incur expenditure in respect of health and safety equipment reasonably required to comply with regulatory and statutory requirements.

Reporting

50. By no later than six months from the date of appointment (and then annually) the Manager must prepare and submit a brief written report to the Tenants, and the Landlord, on the progress of the management of the Property up to that date, providing a copy to the Tribunal at the same time.

End of Appointment

51. No later than 56 days before the end date, the Manager must:

(a) apply to the tribunal for directions as to the disposal of any unexpended monies;

(b) include with that application a brief written report on the progress and outcome of the management of the Property up to that date (a "Final Report"); and

(c) seek a direction from the tribunal as to the mechanism for determining any unresolved disputes arising from the Manager's term of appointment (whether through court or tribunal proceedings or otherwise).

52. Unless the tribunal directs otherwise the Manager must within two months of the end date:

(a) prepare final closing accounts and send copies of the accounts and the Final Report to the Landlord and Tenants, who may raise queries on them within 14 days; and

(b) answer any such queries within a further 14 days.

53. The Manager must reimburse any unexpended monies to the paying parties, or, if it be the case, to any new Tribunal appointed Manager within three months of the end date or, in the case of a dispute, as decided by the Tribunal upon an application by any interested party.

APPENDIX B

First-tier Tribunal Property Chamber
(Residential Property)

Ref no. (for office use only)

Application by a tenant for the appointment of a manager or for the variation or discharge of an order appointing a manager

Section 24 of the Landlord and Tenant Act 1987

It is important that you read the notes below carefully before you complete this form.

This is the correct form to use if you want to ask the Tribunal to appoint a manager under section 24 of the Landlord and Tenant Act 1987, or to discharge or vary an order that has already been made. This form also allows you to ask for a dispensation of the requirement to serve a notice under section 22 of the 1987 Act.

A fee is payable for this application (see section 15 for Help with Fees). The fees are set out in this form.

Applications should be sent as a Microsoft Word document by **email** to the relevant regional tribunal address shown in the Annex to this form. You must also send by email **the documents listed in section 15 of this form**. If you cannot access email or find someone to assist you in lodging your application by email, then a paper application will be acceptable although there may be a delay in dealing with this. Sending an application on paper will not be suitable in urgent cases.

You can now pay the **the fee (if applicable) by an on-line banking payment or by cheque/postal order enclosed with the application form.**

If you want to be sent online banking payment details by email, please tick this box ☐

Please make sure a copy of the application is served on the other party/parties to the application. If you are unable to serve a copy on the other party/parties, please bring this to the tribunal's attention in the covering email or if sending by post in a covering letter.

Please do not send any other documents. When further evidence is needed, you will be asked to send it in separately.

If you have any questions about how to fill in this form, the fee payable, or the procedures the Tribunal will use please contact the appropriate regional office.

If you are completing this form by hand please use BLOCK CAPITAL LETTERS.

1. DETAILS OF APPLICANT(S) (if there are multiple applicants please continue on a separate sheet) – please provide email addresses)

Name:

Address (*including postcode*):

Address for correspondence (*if different from above*):

Telephone:

Day: | *Evening:* | *Mobile:*

Email address: | *Fax:*

Representative name and address, and other contact details: Where details of a representative have been given, all correspondence and communications will be with them until the Tribunal is notified that they are no longer acting for you.

Name:

Reference no. (if any)

Address (*including postcode*):

Telephone:

Day: | *Mobile:*

Email address: | *Fax:*

Note: The Tribunal may copy the application form to other appropriate persons (e.g. other service charge paying leaseholders in the building or development). If you do not want your telephone/fax number or email address to be disclosed to other such persons please omit those details from Box 1 and attach them on a separate sheet.

Where details of a representative have been given, all correspondence and communications will be with them until the Tribunal is notified that they are no longer acting.

2. ADDRESS (including postcode) of SUBJECT PROPERTY (if not already given)

3. BRIEF DESCRIPTION OF BUILDING (*e.g. purpose built block of flats*)

4. DETAILS OF RESPONDENT (S) the person against whom an applicant seeks determination from the tribunal – this will only be the landlord's managing agent if they are a party to the lease. If there are multiple respondents, please continue on a separate sheet.

Name:

Capacity

Address (*including postcode*):

Reference no. (if any)

Address for correspondence (*if different from above*):

Telephone:
Day: *Evening:* *Mobile:*

Email address: *Fax:*

Note: This form asks you to provide the details of parties to the application. (For example the landlord and any management company which owes management obligations to you under your tenancy). Additionally, the Tribunal needs to know the names and addresses of other people who may be significantly affected by the application such as other lessees in the building. Please provide a list of the names, addresses and email addresses of any such person(s). If this is not possible or is impractical, then a written statement should be provided with this application.

5. DETAILS OF LANDLORD (if not already given)

Name

Address (*including postcode*):

Reference no. (if any)

Telephone:

Day: *Evening:* *Mobile:*

Email address: *Fax:*

7. ORDER SOUGHT

Applications where no manager yet appointed by a Court or a Leasehold Valuation Tribunal or the First-tier Tribunal

Are you asking for the Tribunal to appoint a manager? ☐ Yes ☐ No

If so, have you served a section 22 notice? ☐ Yes ☐ No

If not, are you seeking a dispensation? (*see Guidance Note*) ☐ Yes ☐ No

Applications where a manager has previously been appointed by a Court or a Leasehold Valuation Tribunal or the First-tier Tribunal

What is the date of the order appointing a manager and when is the order due to expire?

Do you seek a variation of the order? ☐ Yes ☐ No

Do you want the order to be discharged? ☐ Yes ☐ No

Please complete the section entitled **'GROUNDS FOR APPLICATION'**

Please note: No application for the appointment of a manager may be made to the Tribunal unless a notice under section 22 of the 1987 Act has first been served. Service of such a notice may only be dispensed with by the Tribunal if it is satisfied that it would not be reasonably practicable to serve such a notice.

Leasehold 2 Application by a tenant for the appointment of a manager or for the variation or discharge of an order appointing a manager (05.24)
Page **4** of **10**

8. MANAGER TO BE APPOINTED

If you are making an application to appoint a manager or to vary an order appointing a manager by the substitution of a new manager, please give details of the person you wish to have appointed.

Name

Professional qualification (if any)

Address (including postcode):

Telephone: Fax:

Email address:

9. OTHER APPLICATIONS

Do you know of any other cases involving either: (a) related or similar issues about the management of this property; or (b) the same landlord or tenant or property as in this application? ☐ Yes ☐ No

If Yes, please give details

10. LIMITATION OF COSTS

Some leases allow a landlord to include costs they have incurred in connection with proceedings before a Tribunal (eg. costs of using a professional representative) as part of a service charge. If you want to apply to the Tribunal for those costs to be limited, you need to complete a separate application form – Leasehold 7 (no fee payable).

11. CAN WE DEAL WITH YOUR APPLICATION WITHOUT A HEARING?

If the Tribunal thinks it is appropriate, and all the parties and others notified of their right to attend a hearing consent, it is possible for your application to be dealt with entirely on the basis of written representations and documents and without the need for parties to attend and make oral representations. ('A paper determination').

Please let us know if you would be content with a paper determination if the Tribunal thinks it appropriate. ☐ Yes ☐ No

Note: Even if you have asked for a paper determination the Tribunal may decide that a hearing is necessary. Please complete the remainder of this form on the assumption that a hearing will be held. Where there is to be a hearing, a fee of £220 will become payable by you when you receive notice of the hearing date.

12. TRACK PREFERENCES

We need to decide whether to deal with the case on the Fast Track or the Standard Track (see Guidance Note for an explanation of what a track is). Please let us know which track you think appropriate for this case.

☐ Fast Track
☐ Standard Track

Is there any special reason for urgency in this case? ☐ Yes ☐ No

If Yes, please explain how urgent it is and why:

Note

The Tribunal will normally deal with a case in one of three ways: on paper (see section 11 above) or 'fast track', or 'standard track'. The fast track is designed for cases that need a hearing but are very simple and will not generate a great deal of paperwork or argument. A fast track case will usually be heard within 10 weeks of your application. You should indicate here if you think your case is very simple and can be easily dealt with. The standard track is designed for more complicated cases where there may be numerous issues to be decided or where for example, a lot of documentation is involved. A standard track case may involve the parties being invited to a Case Management Conference which is a meeting at which the steps that need to be taken to bring the case to a final hearing can be discussed.

13. AVAILABILITY

If there are any dates or days we must avoid during the next four months (either for your convenience or the convenience of any expert you may wish to call) please list them here.

Please list the dates on which you will NOT be available:

Leasehold 2 Application by a tenant for the appointment of a manager or for the variation or discharge of an order appointing a manager (05.24)

Page **6** of **10**

14. VENUE REQUIREMENTS

Please provide details of any special requirements you or anyone who will be coming with you may have (e.g. the use of a wheelchair and/or the presence of a translator):

Applications handled by the London regional office are usually heard in Alfred Place, which is fully wheelchair accessible. Elsewhere, hearings are held in local venues which are not all so accessible and the case officers will find it useful to know if you or anyone you want to come to the hearing with you has any special requirements of this kind.

15. CHECKLIST

Please check that you have completed this form fully. The Tribunal will not process your application until this has been done. Please ensure that the following are enclosed with your application and tick the appropriate box to confirm:

A copy of the section 22 notice (if any) is enclosed. ☐

A copy of the previous order appointing a manager (if applicable) is enclosed) ☐

A list of the names and addresses of persons who might be significantly affected by this application is enclosed ☐

EITHER

A crossed cheque or postal order made out to HM Courts and Tribunal Service for the application fee of £110 (if applicable) is enclosed. **Please write your name and address on the back of the cheque or postal order. Please also send a paper copy of your application with your cheque or postal order, regardless of whether you have already emailed the application.** ☐

OR

You have ticked the box at the top of this form to say you want the relevant regional tribunal office to send you details on how to pay the application fee of £110 by on-line banking. **The unique payment reference the tribunal office supplies MUST be used when making your on-line banking payment.**

DO NOT send cash under any circumstances. Cash payment will not be accepted.

Please note where there is to be a hearing, a fee of £220 will become payable by you when you receive notice of the hearing date.

Help with Fees

If you think you may be entitled to a reduced fee, the guide EX160A 'Apply for help with court, tribunal and probate fees' outlines how you can submit an application for Help with Fees.

You can submit your Help with Fees application online at www.gov.uk/help-with-court-fees or by completing the form EX160 'Apply for help with fees'. You can get a copy of the 'Apply for help with fees' form online at www.gov.uk/government/publications/apply-for-help-with-court-and-tribunal-fees or from your regional tribunal office.

If you have completed an online application for Help with Fees please enter the reference number you have been given here.

H	W	F	-					-			

If you have completed form EX160 'Apply for Help with Fees' it must be included with your application.

The 'Apply for help with fees' form will not be copied to other parties.

16. STATEMENT OF TRUTH

The statement of truth must be signed and dated.
I believe that the facts stated in this application are true.

Signed: ______________________ Dated: ______________

GROUNDS FOR APPLICATION

Please use the space below to summarise the ground(s) of your application.

You will be given an opportunity later to give further details of your case and to supply the Tribunal with any documents that support it. At this stage you should give a clear outline of your case so that the Tribunal understands what your application is about. Please continue on a separate sheet if necessary.

Please select as appropriate:

This is an application for the appointment of a manager ☐

and/or

Dispensation from the need to serve a notice under section 22 ☐

An application for the discharge of an order appointing a manager ☐

An application for the variation of an order appointing a manager ☐

Now complete the rest of this form:

The grounds for the application are as follows

ANNEX: Addresses of Tribunal Regional Offices

NORTHERN REGION

HM Courts & Tribunals Service
First-tier Tribunal (Property Chamber) Residential Property, 1st Floor, Piccadilly Exchange, Piccadilly Plaza, Manchester M1 4AH

Telephone: 01612 379491
Fax: 01264 785 128
Email address: RPNorthern@justice.gov.uk

This office covers the following Metropolitan districts: Barnsley, Bolton, Bradford, Bury, Calderdale, Doncaster, Gateshead, Kirklees, Knowsley, Leeds, Liverpool, Manchester, Newcastle-upon-Tyne, Oldham, Rochdale, Rotherham, St. Helens, Salford, Sefton, Sheffield, Stockport, Sunderland, Tameside, Trafford, Tyneside (North & South), Wakefield, Wigan and Wirral.

It also covers the following unitary authorities: Hartlepool, Middlesbrough, Redcar and Cleveland, Darlington, Halton, Blackburn with Darwen, Blackpool, Kingston-upon-Hull, East Riding of Yorkshire, Northeast Lincolnshire, North Lincolnshire, Stockton-on-Tees, Warrington and York.

It also covers the following Counties: Cumbria, Durham, East Cheshire, Lancashire, Lincolnshire, Northumberland, North Yorkshire and West Cheshire.

MIDLAND REGION

HM Courts & Tribunals Service
First-tier Tribunal (Property Chamber) Residential Property, Centre City Tower, 5-7 Hill Street, Birmingham, B5 4UU

Telephone: 0121 600 7888
Fax: 01264 785 122
Email address: RPMidland@justice.gov.uk

This office covers the following Metropolitan districts: Birmingham, Coventry, Dudley, Sandwell, Solihull, Walsall and Wolverhampton.

It also covers the following unitary authorities: Derby, Leicester, Rutland, Nottingham, Herefordshire, Telford and Wrekin and Stoke-on-Trent.

It also covers the following Counties: Derbyshire, Leicestershire, Nottinghamshire, Shropshire, Staffordshire, Warwickshire and Worcestershire.

EASTERN REGION

HM Courts & Tribunals Service
First-tier Tribunal (Property Chamber) Residential Property, Cambridge County Court, 197 East Road Cambridge, CB1 1BA

Telephone: 01223 841 524
Fax: 01264 785 129
Email address: RPEastern@justice.gov.uk

DX 97650 Cambridge 3

This office covers the following unitary authorities: Bracknell Forest, West Berkshire, Reading, Slough, Windsor and Maidenhead, Wokingham, Luton, Peterborough, Milton Keynes, Southend-on-Sea and Thurrock.

It also covers the following Counties: Bedfordshire, Berkshire, Buckinghamshire, Cambridgeshire, Essex, Hertfordshire, Norfolk, Northamptonshire, Oxfordshire and Suffolk.

SOUTHERN REGION

HM Courts & Tribunals Service
First-tier Tribunal (Property Chamber) Residential Property, Havant Justice Centre, The Court House, Elmleigh Road, Havant, Hants, PO9 2AL

Telephone: 01243 779 394
Fax: 0870 7395 900
Email address: RPSouthern@justice.gov.uk

This office covers the following unitary authorities: Bath and Northeast Somerset, Bristol, North Somerset, South Gloucestershire, Bournemouth, Plymouth, Torbay, Poole, Swindon, Medway, Brighton and Hove, Portsmouth, Southampton and the Isle of Wight.

It also covers the following Counties: Cornwall and the Isles of Scilly, Devon, Dorset, East Sussex, Gloucestershire, Hampshire, Kent, Somerset, Surrey, West Sussex and Wiltshire.

LONDON REGION

HM Courts & Tribunals Service
First-tier Tribunal (Property Chamber) Residential Property, 10 Alfred Place, London WC1E 7LR

DX 134205 Tottenham Court Road 2

This office covers all the London boroughs.

Telephone: 020 7446 7700
Fax: 01264 785 060
Email address: London.RAP@justice.gov.uk

The Ministry of Justice and HM Courts and Tribunals Service processes personal information about you in the context of tribunal proceedings.

For details of the standards we follow when processing your data, please visit the following address https://www.gov.uk/government/organisations/hm-courts-and-tribunals-service/about/personal-information-charter

To receive a paper copy of this privacy notice, please call 0300 123 1024/ Textphone 18001 0300 123 1024.

APPENDIX C

LVT8 (See Guidance LVT-G2)

Y Tribiwnlys Eiddo Preswyl
Residential Property Tribunal

Application Form
Section 24 and Section 22 (3) Landlord and Tenant Act 1987

Application for the appointment of a manager or for the variation or discharge of an order appointing a manager under Section 24 of the Landlord and Tenant Act 1987

It is important that you read the notes below carefully before you complete this form.

Please write clearly in BLACK ink and tick boxes where appropriate.

This application form is also available in Welsh. Please contact the tribunal for a Welsh version of this form.

This is the correct form to use if you want to ask the Leasehold Valuation Tribunal to appoint a manager under section 24 of the Landlord and Tenant Act 1987 or to discharge or vary an order that has already been made. This form also allows you to ask for a dispensation of the requirement to serve a notice under section 22 of the 1987 Act.

Documents

You must send the following document(s) ("required document(s)") with this application:

- a copy of the notice of your intention to make this application (if any)
- a copy of the previous order appointing a manager (if applicable)
- a list of names and addresses of all persons who might significantly be affected by this application. This may include other leasees, mortgagees or a superior landlord

Failure to send any required document(s) might may this application invalid.

Please do not send any other documents at this time. If and when further documents, information or evidence are needed, you will be asked to send them separately.

Application Fees

The amount of the application fee will depend on number of dwellings to which the application form relates. To find out how much you will need to pay you should consult the following table:

Number of dwellings to which application relates	Application Fee
5 or fewer dwellings	£150
Between 6 and 10 dwellings	£250
More than 10 dwellings	£350

The fee must be paid by either a crossed cheque or postal order drawn in favour of the "Welsh Government" or by bank transfer, details of which can be provided upon request.

Do not send cash under any circumstances. Cash payment will not be accepted.

LVT8 (See Guidance LVT-G2)

Please note:

- If you do not send the correct fee payable to or in favour of the "Welsh Government" or if you send cash, the application and the cash will be returned to you at your risk.
- A Hearing fee of £150 is also payable when the application is set down for Hearing. If it is not paid by the due date, the application will not proceed to Hearing and may be dismissed or deemed withdrawn.

Waiver of Fees

If the Applicant(s) or the partner(s) of any Applicant(s) is/are in receipt of certain income-related benefits, the Application Fee may be waived or reduced.

To claim a waiver or reduction in the Application Fee, the Applicant(s) in receipt of such benefit or the Applicant(s) whose partner(s) is/are in receipt of such benefit must complete a waiver application form which can be obtained from the Residential Property Tribunal. This will not be copied to the other parties.

Please send the completed application form and the required documents to:

Residential Property Tribunal
Oak House
Cleppa Park
Celtic Springs
Newport
NP10 8BD

Note to Applicants

Applicants are advised that any information that they provide to the Tribunal may be recorded in a decision document. All decisions made by the Tribunal are open to the public.

Language Preference

The Residential Property Tribunal welcomes receiving correspondence in Welsh or English. Any correspondence received in Welsh will be answered in Welsh and corresponding in Welsh will not lead to a delay in responding. The tribunal also welcomes phone calls in Welsh of English.

You may submit forms, documents and make written representations to the tribunal in Welsh or English.

The tribunal will accept applications by email to rpt@gov.wales or in hard copy by post.

Please inform the tribunal of your language preference by completing box 3 below.

LVT8 (See Guidance LVT-G2)

1. DETAILS OF APPLICANT(S) (If there are multiple applicants please continue on a separate sheet)

Name: ______________________________

Address (including postcode): ______________________________

____

____

____

Address for correspondence (if different): ______________________________

____

____

____

Telephone: Day: __________ Evening: __________ Mobile: __________

Email address: ______________________________

Capacity (e.g. Owner): ______________________________

Representative details: ______________________________

____

____

Note: The Tribunal may copy the application form to other appropriate persons (e.g. other service charge paying leaseholders in the building or development). If you are a leaseholder and do not want your telephone number or email address to be disclosed to other such person, please omit those details from Box 1 and attach them on a separate sheet.

Where details of a representative have been given, all correspondence and communication will be through them until the tribunal is notified that they are no longer acting for the applicant(s).

2. PROPERTY ADDRESS (including postcode)

____

____

____

LVT8 (See Guidance LVT-G2)

3. LANGUAGE PREFERENCE

Please indicate your language preference:

Written correspondence? Welsh / English (please delete as appropriate)

Verbal communication? Welsh / English (please delete as appropriate)

Do you wish to speak Welsh in any legal proceedings that may result from this application i.e. tribunal hearing or pre-trial review?

Yes / No (please delete as appropriate)

4. DETAILS OF RESPONDENT(S) (if there are multiple respondents please continue on a separate sheet)

Name: ____________________

Address (including postcode): ____________________

____

____

____

Address for correspondence (if different): ____________________

____

____

____

Telephone: Day: __________ Evening: __________ Mobile: __________

Email address: ____________________

Capacity (e.g. Owner): ____________________

5. DETAILS OF LANDLORD (if not already given)

Name: ____________________

Address (including postcode): ____________________

____

____

____

Telephone: Day: __________ Evening: __________ Mobile: __________

Email address: ____________________

Version 1.1 4

LVT8 (See Guidance LVT-G2)

6. DETAILS OF ANY RECOGNISED TENANTS' ASSOCIATIONS

Name: ______________________

Address (including postcode): ______________________

____

____

____

Telephone: Day: __________ Evening: __________ Mobile: __________

Email address: ______________________

7. ORDER SOUGHT

Applications where no manager yet appointed by a Court or Tribunal

Are you asking the Tribunal to appoint a manager? YES ☐ NO ☐

If so, have you served a section 22 notice? YES ☐ NO ☐

If not, are you seeking a dispensation? YES ☐ NO ☐

No application for the appointment of a manager may be made unless a notice under section 22 of the 1987 Act has first been served. Service of such a notice may only be dispensed with by the Tribunal if it is satisfied that it would not be reasonably practicable to serve such a notice.

Applications where a manager has previously been appointed by a Court or Tribunal

What is the date of the order appointing a manager ______________________

Do you seek a variation of the order? YES ☐ NO ☐

Do you want the order to be discharged? YES ☐ NO ☐

LVT8 (See Guidance LVT-G2)

8. GROUNDS OF APPLICATION

Please provide a clear outline of your case so that the Tribunal understands what your application is about. You will be given an opportunity to give further details of your case at a later date.

Please continue on a separate sheet if necessary.

LVT8 (See Guidance LVT-G2)

9. MANAGER TO BE APPOINTED

If you are making an application to appoint a manager, or to vary an order appointing a manager by the substitution of a new manager, please give details of the person you wish to have appointed.

Name: ______________________________

Address (including postcode): ______________________________

____

____

____

Telephone: Day: Evening: Mobile:

10. OTHER APPLICATIONS

Do you know of any other cases involving either:

(a) related or similar issues about the management of this property; or

(b) the same landlord or tenant or property as in this application?

If so, please give details

____

____

____

11. LIMITATION OF COSTS

If you are a tenant, do you wish to make a Section 20C application? (See note below)

YES ☐ NO ☐

If so, why?

____

____

____

____

Note: some leases allow a landlord to include costs incurred in connection with proceedings before a Tribunal as part of a service charge. Section 20C of the Landlord and Tenant Act 1985 gives the Tribunal power, on application by the tenant, to make an order to the effect that such costs are not to be treated as relevant costs to be taken into account in determining the amount of any service charge payable by the tenant or any other person(s) specified in the application. If you are a tenant you should indicate here whether you want the Tribunal to consider making such an order.

If you are a tenant and this application has been made by another party, you may nonetheless ask the Tribunal to make an Order under Section 20C. If so please write to the Tribunal asking it to make such an Order and set out the reasons why.

LVT8 (See Guidance LVT-G2)

12. CAN WE DEAL WITH YOUR APPLICATION WITHOUT A HEARING?

It is possible for your application to be dealt with entirely on the basis of written representations ("paper determination") but only if:

- the Tribunal thinks it is appropriate
- all parties agree

Even if you agree to a paper determination

- the Tribunal may nonetheless decide that an oral hearing is necessary
- you or any other party may still ask for an oral hearing at any time before the determination is made

Do you agree to this application being determined without an oral hearing YES ☐ NO ☐

Please ensure that you complete this form in full on the assumption that there will be an oral hearing.

13. AVAILABILITY

If there are any days or dates we must avoid during the next three months please list them here.

Dates on which you will **NOT** be available:

____

____

____

____

14. VENUE REQUIREMENTS

Please provide details of any special requirements you or anyone who will be coming with you may have (e.g. wheelchair access/or the presence of an interpreter). It will assist the Tribunal in making the arrangements if it has been made aware of your needs.

____

____

____

____

Version 1.1 8

LVT8 (See Guidance LVT-G2)

15. STATEMENT OF TRUTH
I believe that the facts stated in this application are true.
Signed: ______________________
Name (IN CAPITALS): ______________________
Capacity (e.g. Owner): ______________________
Date: ______________________

CHECKLIST

Please check that:

- you have completed this form IN FULL
- you have enclosed the required documents

The Tribunal will not process your application if you have not done so.

Please contact the Residential Property Tribunal if you have any questions about how to fill in this form or the procedures the Tribunal will use:

Telephone: 0300 025 2777
Email: rpt@gov.wales

MORE BOOKS BY LAW BRIEF PUBLISHING

A selection of our other titles available now:-

'A Practical Guide to Probation Breaches and Other Applications' by Mark Thomas
'A Practical Guide to Remarriage and Divorce' by Cordelia Williams & Claire Howard
'A Practical Guide to Privacy, Transparency, Reporting Restrictions and Closed Proceedings in the Court of Protection' by Laura Mannering
'Beaumont on Barristers – A Guide to Defending Disciplinary Proceedings (Second Edition)' by Marc Beaumont
'A Practical Guide to Payments for Environmental Services' by Ben Sharples
'A Practical Guide to the Law of Pregnancy and Maternity at Work' by Rebecca Thomas
'A Practical Guide to Redundancy – Second Edition' by Philip Hyland & Collette Moore
'A Practical Guide to International Issues for Scottish Family Lawyers' by Susie Mountain, Donna McKay, Ken MacDonald
'A Practical Guide to the Law on Deprivation of Liberty' by Ben Troke
'A Practical Guide to Rights over Airspace and Subsoil – Second Edition' by Daniel Gatty
'A Practical Guide to the Law in Relation to Inquests' by Ramya Nagesh
'A Practical Guide to the Construction and Rectification of Wills and Trust Instruments (Second Edition)' by Edward Hewitt
'A Practical Guide to Data Protection in Social Housing' by Clare Paterson
'A Practical Guide to Spousal Maintenance – Second Edition' by Liz Cowell
'A Practical Guide to International Parental Child Abduction Law (England and Wales)' by Dr Onyója Momoh
'A Practical Guide to Deprivation of British Citizenship' by Sean Ell
'A Practical Guide to Commercial Property Service Charges' by Rachel Garton
'A Practical Guide to Clinical Negligence – Third Edition' by Geoffrey Simpson-Scott (Geoff)
'A Practical Guide to the Rights of Grandparents in Children Proceedings – Second Edition' by Stuart Barlow

'The Electronic Communications Code: A Practical Guide – Second Edition' by Kerry Bretherton KC, James Castle, Mark Loveday
'A Practical Guide to the Independent School Standards – September 2023 Edition' by Sarah McKimm
'A Practical Guide to Estate Administration and Crypto Assets' by Richard Marshall
'A Practical Guide to Parental Alienation in Private and Public Law Children Cases' by Sam King QC & Frankie Shama
'Contested Heritage – Removing Art from Land and Historic Buildings' by Richard Harwood QC, Catherine Dobson, David Sawtell
'The Limits of Separate Legal Personality: When Those Running a Company Can Be Held Personally Liable for Losses Caused to Third Parties Outside of the Company' by Dr Mike Wilkinson
'A Practical Guide to Transgender Law' by Robin Moira White & Nicola Newbegin
'A Practical Guide to 'Stranded Spouses' in Family Law' by Mani Singh Basi
'A Practical Guide to Residential Freehold Conveyancing' by Lorraine Richardson
'A Practical Guide to Pensions on Divorce for Lawyers' by Bryan Scant
'A Practical Guide to Challenging Sham Marriage Allegations in Immigration Law' by Priya Solanki
'A Practical Guide to Digital Communications Evidence in Criminal Law' by Sam Willis
'A Practical Guide to Legal Rights in Scotland' by Sarah-Jane Macdonald
'A Practical Guide to New Build Conveyancing' by Paul Sams & Rebecca East
'A Practical Guide to Inherited Wealth on Divorce' by Hayley Trim
'A Practical Guide to Practice Direction 12J and Domestic Abuse in Private Law Children Proceedings' by Rebecca Cross & Malvika Jaganmohan
'A Practical Guide to Confiscation and Restraint' by Narita Bahra QC, John Carl Townsend, David Winch
'A Practical Guide to the Law of Forests in Scotland' by Philip Buchan
'A Practical Guide to Health and Medical Cases in Immigration Law' by Rebecca Chapman & Miranda Butler
'A Practical Guide to Bad Character Evidence for Criminal Practitioners by Aparna Rao
'A Practical Guide to Extradition Law post-Brexit' by Myles Grandison et al
'A Practical Guide to Hoarding and Mental Health for Housing Lawyers' by Rachel Coyle

'Stephens on Contractual Indemnities' by Richard Stephens
'A Practical Guide to the EU Succession Regulation' by Richard Frimston
'A Practical Guide to Solicitor and Client Costs – Second Edition' by Robin Dunne
'Constructive Dismissal – Practice Pointers and Principles' by Benjimin Burgher
'A Practical Guide to Religion and Belief Discrimination Claims in the Workplace' by Kashif Ali
'A Practical Guide to the Law of Medical Treatment Decisions' by Ben Troke
'Fundamental Dishonesty and QOCS in Personal Injury Proceedings: Law and Practice' by Jake Rowley
'A Practical Guide to the Law in Relation to School Exclusions' by Charlotte Hadfield & Alice de Coverley
'A Practical Guide to Divorce for the Silver Separators' by Karin Walker
'The Right to be Forgotten – The Law and Practical Issues' by Melissa Stock
'A Practical Guide to Planning Law and Rights of Way in National Parks, the Broads and AONBs' by James Maurici QC, James Neill et al
'A Practical Guide to Election Law' by Tom Tabori
'A Practical Guide to the Law in Relation to Surrogacy' by Andrew Powell
'A Practical Guide to Claims Arising from Fatal Accidents – Second Edition' by James Patience
'A Practical Guide to Asbestos Claims' by Jonathan Owen & Gareth McAloon
'A Practical Guide to Stamp Duty Land Tax in England and Northern Ireland' by Suzanne O'Hara
'A Practical Guide to the Law of Farming Partnerships' by Philip Whitcomb
'A Practical Guide to the Law of Unlawful Eviction and Harassment – Second Edition' by Stephanie Lovegrove
'A Practical Guide to Costs in Personal Injury Claims – Second Edition' by Matthew Hoe
'A Practical Guide to the General Data Protection Regulation (GDPR) – Second Edition' by Keith Markham
'A Practical Guide to Working with Litigants in Person and McKenzie Friends in Family Cases' by Stuart Barlow
'Protecting Unregistered Brands: A Practical Guide to the Law of Passing Off' by Lorna Brazell
'A Practical Guide to Secondary Liability and Joint Enterprise Post-Jogee' by Joanne Cecil & James Mehigan

'A Practical Guide to the Pre-Action RTA Claims Protocol for Personal Injury Lawyers' by Antonia Ford
'A Practical Guide to Neighbour Disputes and the Law' by Alexander Walsh
'A Practical Guide to Coercive Control for Legal Practitioners and Victims' by Rachel Horman
'A Practical Guide to the Law of Driverless Cars – Second Edition'
by Alex Glassbrook, Emma Northey & Scarlett Milligan
'A Practical Guide to TOLATA Claims' by Greg Williams
'A Practical Guide to Elderly Law – Second Edition' by Justin Patten
'A Practical Guide to Responding to Housing Disrepair and Unfitness Claims' by Iain Wightwick
'A Practical Guide to the Law of Bullying and Harassment in the Workplace' by Philip Hyland
'How to Be a Freelance Solicitor: A Practical Guide to the SRA-Regulated Freelance Solicitor Model' by Paul Bennett
'A Practical Guide to Prison Injury Claims' by Malcolm Johnson
'A Practical Guide to Advising Clients at the Police Station' by Colin Stephen McKeown-Beaumont
'A Practical Guide to Antisocial Behaviour Injunctions – Second Edition' by Iain Wightwick
'Practical Mediation: A Guide for Mediators, Advocates, Advisers, Lawyers, and Students in Civil, Commercial, Business, Property, Workplace, and Employment Cases' by Jonathan Dingle with John Sephton
'The Mini-Pupillage Workbook' by David Boyle
'A Practical Guide to Crofting Law' by Brian Inkster
'A Practical Guide to the Law of Domain Names and Cybersquatting' by Andrew Clemson
'A Practical Guide to the Law of Gender Pay Gap Reporting' by Harini Iyengar
'NHS Whistleblowing and the Law' by Joseph England
'Employment Law and the Gig Economy' by Nigel Mackay & Annie Powell
'A Practical Guide to Noise Induced Hearing Loss (NIHL) Claims' by Andrew Mckie, Ian Skeate, Gareth McAloon
'An Introduction to Beauty Negligence Claims – A Practical Guide for the Personal Injury Practitioner' by Greg Almond
'Intercompany Agreements for Transfer Pricing Compliance' by Paul Sutton
'Zen and the Art of Mediation' by Martin Plowman
'A Practical Guide to Adoption for Family Lawyers' by Graham Pegg

www.ingramcontent.com/pod-product-compliance
Lightning Source LLC
LaVergne TN
LVHW022104200926
848481LV00003B/1060
* 9 7 8 1 9 1 6 6 9 8 8 6 4 *